# The Gheraṇḍa Saṁhitā

This fine edition of the Gheranda Samhita is a very readable English translation. A seventeenth century classical manual, it speaks of a seven fold yoga and is considered the most detailed of the three classical texts of the Hatha yoga. *Gheranda Saṁhitā* is a manual of yoga taught by Gheranda to his disciple Chanda Kapali. Unlike other Hatha yoga texts, the Gheranda Samhita speaks of a sevenfold yoga: *Shatkarma* for purification, *Asana* for strengthening, *Mudra* for steadying, *Pratyahara* for calming, *Pranayama* for lightness, *Dhyana* for perception and *Samadhi* for isolation.

# The Gheraṇḍa Saṁhitā

*Translated into English by*

Srisa Chandra Vasu

DEV PUBLISHERS
New Delhi

*Published by:*

DEV PUBLISHERS & DISTRIBUTORS

2nd Floor, Prakash Deep,
22, Delhi Medical Association Road,
Darya Ganj,
New Delhi-110002
Phone : 011-4357 2647
e-mail: devbooks@hotmail.com
website: www.devbooks.co.in

ISBN 978-93-81406-20-5
This edition 2013
Reprint 2026



Printed in India

# CONTENTS

## Lesson 2

**The Āsanas, or Postures 16**



## Lesson 3

**On Mudrās 29**

## Lesson 4



## Lesson 5



## Lesson 6



## Lesson 7

# Foreword

Gheraṇḍa Saṁhitā is a Tāntrika work, treating of Haṭha-Yoga. It consists of a dialogue between the sage Gheraṇḍa and an enquirer called Caṇḍa Kāpāli. The book is divided into seven lessons or Chapters and comprises, in all, some three hundred and fifty verses. It closely follows in the foot-steps of the famous treatise on Haṭha-Yoga, known as Haṭha-Yoga Pradīpikā. In fact, a large number of verses of Gheraṇḍa Saṁhitā correspond *verbatim* with those of the Pradīpikā. It may, therefore, be presumed that one has borrowed from the other, or both have drawn from a common source.

The book teaches Yoga under seven heads or Sādhanas. The first gives directions for the purification of the Body (inside and out). The second relates to Postures, the third to Mudrās, the fourth to Pratyā-hāra, the fifth to Prāṇāyāma, the sixth to Dhyāna, and the seventh to Samādhi. These are taught successively—a chapter being devoted to each (see Ch. I, v, 9-11).

The theory of Haṭha-Yoga, to put it broadly, is that concentration or Samādhi can be attained by purification of the physical body and certain physical exercises. The relation between physical shell (*ghaṭa*) and mind is so complete and subtle, and their interaction is so curious and so much enveloped in mystery, that it is not strange that Haṭha-Yogīs should have imagined that certain physical training will induce certain mental transformations.

Another explanation—and a later one—is that Haṭha-Yoga means the Yoga or union between ha (ह) and ṭha (ठ); the ह meaning the sun; and ठ the moon; or the union of the Prāṇa and the Apāna Vāyus. This is also a physical process carried to a higher plane.

The first question, which an unprejudiced enquirer will naturally put, after perusing this book, will be, are all these things possible? and do these practices produce the result attributed to them?

As to the possibility of these practices, there can be no doubt. They do not violate any anatomical or physiological facts. The practices, some of them at least, may appear revolting and disgusting, but they are not *per se* impossible. Moreover, many of my readers may have come across persons who can practically illustrate these. Such persons are by no means rare in India. Every place of pilgrimage, such as Benares and Allahabad, contains several of them, in various stages of progress. My own Guru showed me and all his visitors at Allahabad and Meerut several of these processes, and taught some people how to do them themselves. The difficult processes, such as Vāri-Sāra (Ch. I.17), Agni-Sāra (I.20), Daṇḍa-Dhauti (I.37), Vāsa-Dhauti (I.40), etc. were all shown by him; so also the various Vastis, Neti, Āsanas, etc. Many of these may be classified as gymnastic exercises; their performers need not always be holy or saint-like personages. Several jugglers have been known to perform various Āsanas and Mudrās, and earn their livelihood by showing them to the public. For persons whose muscles have become stiffened and the bones hardened by age, the acquirement of several of these postures, etc. is next to impossible; and it is better that they should not court failure or disappointment by attempting these at an advanced age. But Prāṇāyāma (regulation of breath), Dhāraṇā and Dhyāna are possible for all.

As to the utility of these processes, genuine doubts may be entertained. Many of them may appear puerile, and, if not positively injurious, at least, useless. Although it is not possible within the short space at my command, to give the rationale of *all* these practices, and to justify them to a doubting public, yet I shall briefly illustrate the advantages of some of them. Thus, to begin with *Vāta-sāra* (I.15). It is the process of filling the stomach with air, and expelling the wind through the posterior passage. The greatest duct or canal in the human body is the alimentary canal, beginning with the oesophagus (throat) and ending with the rectum. It is some twenty-six feet in length. This great drain contains all the rubbish of the body. Nature periodically cleanses it. Yoga practice makes that cleansing thorough and voluntary. If the cleansing is incomplete, then the foetid matters putrify in the stomach and intestines, and generate noxious and deleterious gases which cause diseases. Now *Vāta-sāra* by passing a current of air through the canal, causes the oxidation of the foetid products of the body; and thus conduces to health, and increases digestion. In fact, it gives a tone to the whole system. Similarly, *Vāri-sāra* is flushing the canal with water, instead of air. It thoroughly purges the whole canal; and does the same work as an aperient or a purgative, but with ten times more efficacy and without the injurious effects of these drugs. A person, knowing *Vāta-sāra* and *Vāri-sāra*, stands in no need of purgatives: the same may be said of Bahiṣkṛta Dhauti (I.22). By Agnisāra (I.20), the nerves and muscles of the stomach are brought under the control of volition; and by the gentle shaking of the stomach and the intestines, these organs lose their lethargy, and act with greater vigour. The washing taught in I.23, 24, is a little dangerous, and may lead to prolapsus, and, a person who can do *Vāri-sāra* need not do this. The advantages of cleaning the teeth and the tongue are obvious, and, need not be dilated upon. The lengthening of the tongue (I.32) is necessary for performing hyber-nation. In doing this, man but imitates the lower creation, like frogs, etc. who in hybernating turn their tongues upward, closing the respiratory passage. Perhaps, the most interesting of all Dhautis is the Vāsa-Dhauti (I.41), which has led unobservant persons to the belief that the Yogīs can bring out the intestines by the mouth, wash them, and then swallowing them again place them in their proper position. This Dhauti is, however, a very simple process, and by so doing the mucus, phlegm, etc. adhering to the sides of the alimentary canal are removed. Water and air could not remove these viscid substances that stick to the sides of the canal.

The Neti, an easy process, clears the nostrils; and cures the tendency or predisposition to cold and catarrh. The Kapālabhāti (I.55) is a means of cleansing the frontal sinus, said to be the seat of Intelligence. This hollow cannot be directly reached from the outside, but by this process of Kapālabhāti, the nerves surrounding it and spreading over the forehead are brought into play and invigorated.

The various Āsanas taught in Chapter II are gymnastic exercises, good for general health and peace of mind, and calming of passions. The thirty-two Āsanas taught in this book are not all of equal efficacy or importance. Padmāsana is generally approved by all. The others may be practised occasionally for variation and recreation. Some of these postures help in checking animal passions by causing atrophy of the nerves of particular places. Others by straining and stretching of certain muscles create a pleasant sensation of strength and refreshment. The Āsanas are antidotes to the sedentary contemplation of Yoga—a habit which may otherwise lead to mental hallucinations and nervous disorders.

The Mudrās are similar to Āsanas in their action and efficacy. The gazing taught in some of these induces hypnotic sleep; and the Bandhas, by closing all the exits for air, produce a tension within the system, generating thereby a sort of electric current or force, called Kuṇḍalanī Śakti. It is this Śakti which is the helpmate of the Yogīs in performing their wonders. The Khecarī Mudrā (III. 25-27) causes levitation of the body. That levitation is possible has now been established beyond doubt. What the particular conditions are, under which this takes place, has not yet been fully investigated by Western Science; but that the restraining of breath is one of these conditions may be said to be an undoubted truth. The Śakticālana is a mysterious process, and until a person practically realises it, he can hardly believe it. The Mudrās are mixed physical and mental processes, a bridge between Āsanas and Pratyāhāra.

The subject of Pratyāhāra is treated in Chapter IV in five ślokas. It is the process of restraining the mind from wandering, and restricting it to a fixed idea. All the five senses must be controlled, and they should not be allowed to divert the attention.

Prāṇāyāma is the Haṭha-Yoga *par excellence.* It is as dangerous when practised without the supervision of a competent teacher, as it is useful when practised under his supervision. To quote the words of a great authority on this subject: "By practising it according to rule, all diseases are destroyed; but by doing so irregularly, all diseases are generated, such as hiccough, asthma, cough, head-ache, ear-ache, diseases of the eye, etc." A practical Guru is absolutely necessary to teach Prāṇāyāma: the directions given in this book are useful as subsidiary rules. Many mistakes and dangers will, however, be warded off by a strict adherence to these rules. The place—a small and solitary cell; the time—spring and autumn; the food—light and sātvika; these are some of the important preliminaries. Over-exertion, fasting, etc. should be avoided (V.30). This shows clearly that Haṭha-Yoga is not to be confounded with asceticism. It is far from that. As the training of an athlete is not asceticism; so that of a Haṭha-Yogī is far from being so. True, celibacy is a necessary condition for both, but then that alone does not constitute asceticism. The directions regarding food are peculiar for the people of Bengal, the author of this treatise being apparently a Vaiṣṇava of Bengal. For other countries and persons, these directions may not be applicable in their entirety. But animal food, intoxicating liquors, tobacco, and drugs are strictly prohibited for all climes.

There are three parts of Prāṇāyāma—Pūraka or drawing in of the breath; Kumbhaka or retaining the breath; and Recaka or expelling the breath. The proportion of these should be 1 : 4 : 2, *i.e.*. if Pūraka takes 12 seconds, Kumbhaka should be 48 seconds, and Recaka 24 seconds. The ratio being kept the same, the period of retention, etc. may be increased *ad infinitum.* The beginner should proceed cautiously, and should not increase the periods of 16 : 64 : 32 seconds. He should carefully note the various mental and physical changes going on in his system while practising it. Perspiration should be wiped off with a dry towel: nor should he be afraid when he begins to feel a sort of quiver all over the body. Sometimes he may be jerked off his seat, sometimes he may involuntarily jump about the room like a frog. These should not frighten him. Sometimes there may be no physical manifestations, but mental reactions. He may hear noises, see visions, smell strange odours, or taste delightful delicacies. These are for the most part hallucinations, indicating an excited state of the nervous system. These will soon go off of themselves when not attended to. But flashes of truth will also illumine his heart now and then. Sometimes in the Cidākāśa, he may see reflected distant scenes and events, thoughts of persons will become visible to him; and he himself may leave his body and be carried in space with incalculable velocity. All these symptoms accompany Prāṇāyāma. The Guru must always be near at hand to help and control; for otherwise insanity and not clairvoyance may be the outcome of all this. These are the results of higher stages of Prāṇāyāma. But every person may practise this for two or three minutes, and experience its beneficial results on his own body. Petty disorders, like head-ache, stomach-ache, chill before fever, weariness of body and mind will vanish instantaneously by performing two or three Kumbhakas. Some persons are born with the faculty of performing Prāṇāyāma—Swedenbourg was a living example of this in the West. All persons unconsciously perform Prāṇāyāma when absorbed in deep thinking.

The ten Vāyus (V.60) are the various nervous forces or currents of the human body.

The various sorts of Kumbhakas taught in Chapter V do not require much elucidation. The Bhrāmarī Kumbhaka (V. 77), however, is a little peculiar. It leads one to hear the various sounds called Anāhata. These sounds are said to be caused within the body by the rushing of the blood through the arteries and veins. The fixing of mind on these sounds soon produces trance.

Dhyāna and Samādhi are purely mental processes. Fixity and one-pointedness of attention produce trance. The experiments of hypnotism prove this. To fix the mind on one idea produces exaltation of mental faculties.

**S.C.V.**

# Lesson 1

## प्रथमोपदेशः

## On the Training of the Physical Body

SALUTATION

I bow to that Lord Primeval who taught in the beginning the science of the Training in Hardiness (Haṭha Yoga)—a science that stands out as the first rung on the ladder that leads to the supreme heights of Royal Training (Rāja. Yoga).

*Note*—The Training of the body is the first step to the training of the mind. A healthy mind can exist only in a healthy body. Hence the Haṭha Yoga or training of the body is the first step to the training of the mind or Rāja Yoga. Haṭha may be translated as "hard" or the training of or in Hardiness. Rāja in this connection may be translated as royal or softness, or training in royal graces or mental discipline.

**घटस्थयोगकथनम्**

**एकदा चण्डकापालिर्गत्वा घेरण्डकुट्टिरम्।**
**प्रणम्य विनयाद्भक्त्या घेरण्डं परिपृच्छति॥ १॥**

**1.** Once Caṇḍa Kāpāli going to the cottage of Gheraṇḍa saluted him with reverence and devotion.

**श्रीचण्डकापालिरुवाच**

**घटस्थयोगं योगेश तत्वज्ञानस्य कारणम्।**
**इदानीं श्रोतुमिच्छामि योगेश्वर वद प्रभो॥ २॥**

Caṇḍa Kāpāli said :

**2.** O Master of Yoga! O best of the Yogins! O Lord! I wish now to learn the Physical Discipline (Yoga), which leads to the knowledge of truth (or Tattva-jñāna).

**घेरण्ड उवाच**

**साधु साधु महाबाहो यन्मान्त्वं परिपृच्छसि।**
**कथयामि हि ते वत्स सावधानावधारय॥ ३॥**

GHERAṆḌA REPLIED

**3.** Well asked, indeed, O mighty armed, I shall tell thee, O child, what thou askest me. Attend to it with diligence.

**नास्ति मायासमः पाशो नास्ति योगात्परं बलम्।**
**नास्तिज्ञानात्परो बन्धुर्नाहङ्कारात् परो रिपुः॥ ४॥**

**4.** There are no fetters like those of Illusion (Māyā), no strength like that which comes from discipline (Yoga), there is no friend higher than knowledge (Jñāna), and no greater enemy than Egoism (Ahaṅkāra).

**अभ्यासात्कादिवर्णानि यथा शास्त्राणि बोधयेत्।**
**तथा योगं समासाद्य तत्त्वज्ञानञ्च लभ्यते॥ ५॥**

**5.** As by learning the alphabets one can, through practice, master all the sciences, so by thoroughly practising first the (physical) training, one acquires the Knowledge of the True.

**सुकृतैर्दुष्कृतैः कार्यैर्जायते प्राणिनां घटः।**
**घटादुत्पद्यते कर्म्म घटियन्त्रं यथा भ्रमेत्॥ ६॥**

**6.** On account of good and bad deeds, the bodies of all animated beings are produced, and the bodies give rise to works (Karma which leads to rebirth) and thus the circle is continued like that of a Persian Wheel.

ऊर्ध्वाधो भ्रमते यद्वद्घटियन्त्रं गवां वशात्।
तद्वत्कर्म्मवशाज्जीवो भ्रमते जन्ममृत्युभिः॥ ७॥

**7.** As the Persian Wheel in drawing water from a well goes up and down, moved by the bullocks (filling and exhausting the buckets again and again), so the sonl passes through life and death moved by its Deeds.

आमकुम्भ इवाम्भस्थो जीर्यमाणः सदा घटः।
योगानलेन संदह्य घटशुद्धिं समाचरेत्॥ ८॥

**8.** Like unto an unbaked earthen pot thrown in water, the body is soon decayed (in this world). Bake it hard in the fire of Training in order to strengthen and purify the body.

अथ सप्तसाधनम्

शोधनं दृढता चैव स्थैर्य्यं धैर्य्यञ्च लाघवम्।
प्रत्यक्षञ्च निर्लिप्तञ्च घटस्य सप्तसाधनम्॥ ९॥

THE SEVEN EXERCISES

**9.** The seven exercises which appertain to this Training of the body are the following :—Purificatory, strengthening, steadying, calming, and those leading to lightness, perception, and isolation.

अथ सप्तसाधनलक्षणम्

षट्कर्मणां शोधनञ्च आसनेन भवेद्दृढम्।
मुद्रया स्थिरता चैव प्रत्याहारेण धीरता॥ १०॥
प्राणायामाल्लाघवञ्च ध्यानात्प्रत्यक्षमात्मनि।
समाधिना निर्लिप्तञ्च मुक्तिरेव न संशयः॥ ११॥

**10–11.** 1st—The purification is acquired by the regular performance of six practices (to be mentioned shortly); 2nd—Āsana or posture gives Dṛḍhatā or strength; 3rd—Mudrā gives Sthiratā or steadiness; 4th—Pratyāhāra gives Dhairyatā or calmness; 5th—

Prāṇāyāma gives lightness or Laghimā; 6th—Dhyāna gives perception (Pratyakṣatva) of Self; and 7th—Samādhi gives isolation (Nirliptatā), which is verily the Freedom.

अथ शोधनम्

धौतिर्बस्तिस्तथा नेतिर्लौलिकी त्राटकं तथा।
कपालभातिश्चैतानि षट्कर्म्माणि समाचरेत्॥ १२॥

THE SIX PURIFICATORY PROCESSES

**12.** (1) Dhauti; (2) Basti; (3) Neti; (4) Laukikī; (5) Trāṭaka; (6) Kapālabhāti are the Ṣaṭkarmas or six practices, known as Sādhana.

---

PART I

अथ धौतिः

अन्तर्धौतिर्दन्तधौतिर्हृद्धौतिर्मूलशोधनम्।
धौतिं चतुर्विधां कृत्वा घटं कुर्वन्तु निर्मलम्॥ १३॥

THE FOUR INTERNAL DHAUTIS

**13.** The Dhautis are of four kinds, and they clear away the impurities of the body. They are:—(a) Antardhauti (internal washing); (b) Dantadhauti (cleaning the teeth); (c) Hṛddhauti cleaning the heart); (d) Mūlaśodhana (cleaning the rectum).

अथ अन्तर्धौतिः

वातसारं वारिसारं वह्निसारं बहिष्कृतम्।
घटस्य निर्म्मलार्थाय अन्धौंतिश्चतुर्विधा॥ १४॥

ANTAR-DHAUTI

**14.** Antardhauti is again sub-divided into four parts :—Vātasāra (wind purification), Vārisāra (water purification), Vahnisāra (fire purification), and Bahiṣkṛta.

अथ वातसारः
काकचञ्चूवदास्येन पिबेद्वायुं शनैः शनैः।
चालयेदुदरं पश्चाद्वर्त्मना रेचयेच्छनैः॥ १५॥

(*a*[1]) VĀTASĀRA-DHAUTI

**15.** Contract the mouth like the beak of a crow and drink air slowly, and filling the stomach slowly with it, move it therein, and then slowly force it out through the lower passage.

वातसारं परं गोप्यं देहनिर्म्मलकारणम्।
सर्वरोगक्षयकरं देहानलविवर्द्धकम्॥ १६॥

**16.** The Vātasāra is a very secret process, it causes the purification of the body, it destroys all diseases and increases the gastric-fire.

अथ वारिसारः
आकण्ठं पूरयेद्वारि वक्त्रेण च पिबेच्छनैः।
चालयेदुदरेणैव चोदराद्रेचयेदधः॥ १७॥

(*a*[2]) VĀRISĀRA-DHAUTI

**17.** Fill the mouth with water down to the throat, and then drink it slowly; and then move it through the stomach, forcing it downwards expelling it through the rectum.

वारिसारं परं गोप्यं देहनिर्म्मलकारकम्।
साधयेत्तत्प्रयत्नेन देवदेहं प्रपद्यते॥ १८॥

**18.** This process should be kept very secret. It purifies the body. And by practising it with care, one gets a luminous or shining body.

वारिसारं परां धौतिं साधयेद्यः प्रयत्नतः।
मलदेहं शोधयित्वा देवदेहं प्रपद्यते॥ १९॥

**19.** The Vārisāra is the highest Dhauti. He who practises it with ease, purifies his filthy body and turns it into a shining one.

अथ अग्निसारः

नाभिग्रन्थिं मेरुपृष्ठे शतवारञ्च कारयेत्।
अग्निसारमेषा धौतिर्योगिना योगसिद्धिदा॥ २०॥

(*a*³) AGNISĀRA OR FIRE PURIFICATION

**20.** Press in the naval knot or intestines towards the spine for one hundred times. This is Agnisāra or fire process. This gives success in the practice of Yoga, it cures all the diseases of the stomach (gastric juice) and increases the internal fire.

उदरामयजंत्यक्त्वा जठराग्निं विवर्धयेत्।
एषा धौतिः परा गोप्या देवानामपि दुर्लभा।
केवलं धौतिमात्रेण देवदेहो भवेद्ध्रुवम्॥ २१॥

**21.** This form of Dhauti should be kept very secret, and it is hardly to be attained even by the gods. By this Dhauti alone one certainly gets a luminous body.

अथ बहिष्कृतधौतिः

काकीमुद्रां साधयित्वा पूरयेदुदरं मरुत्।
धारयेदर्द्धयामन्तु चालयेदर्धवर्त्मना।
एषा धौतिः परागोप्या न प्रकाश्या कदाचन॥ २२॥

(*a*⁴) BĀHIṢKṚTA-DHAUTI

**22.** By Kākacañcu or crow-bill Mudrā fill the stomach with air, hold it there for one hour and a half, and then force it down towards the intestines. This Dhauti must be kept a great secret, and must not be revealed to anybody.

अथ प्रक्षालनम्

नाभिमग्नो जले स्थित्वा शक्तिनाडीं विसर्जयेत्।
कराभ्यां क्षालयेन्नाडीं यावन्मलविसर्जनम्।
तावत्प्रक्षाल्य नाडीञ्च उदरे वेशयेत् पुनः॥ २३॥

**23.** Then standing in navel-deep water, draw out the Śaktināḍī (long intestines), wash the Nāḍī with hand, and so long as its filth is not all washed away, wash it with care, and then draw it in again into the abdomen.

इदं प्रक्षालनं गोप्यं देवानामपि दुर्लभम्।
केवलं धौतिमात्रेण देवदेहो भवेद्ध्रुवम्॥ २४॥

**24.** This process should be kept secret. It is not easily to be attained even by the gods. Simply by this Dhauti one gets Deva-deha. (Godlike body.)

अथ बहिष्कृतधौतिप्रयोगः

यामार्धं धारणां शक्तिं यावन्न साधयेन्नरः ।
वहिष्कृतं महद्धौतिस्तावच्चैव न जायते॥ २५॥

**25.** As long as a person has not the power of retaining the breath for an hour and a half (or retaining wind in the stomach for that period), so long he cannot achieve this grand Dhauti or purification, known as Bahiṣkṛtadhauti.

अथ दन्तधौतिः

दन्तमूलं जिह्वामूलं रन्ध्रञ्च कर्णयुग्मयोः।
कपालरन्ध्रं पञ्चैते दन्तधौतिं विधीयते॥ २६॥

*(b)* DANTA-DHAUTI, OR TEETH PURIFICATION

**26.** Danta-Dhauti is of five kinds : purification of the teeth, of the root of the tongue, of the two holes of the ear, and of the frontal-sinuses.

अथ दन्तमूलधौतिः

खदिरेण रसेनाथ मृत्तिकया च शुद्धया।
मार्जयेद्दन्तमूलञ्च यावत्किल्बिषमाहरेत्॥ २७॥

*(b¹)* DANTA-MŪLA-DHAUTI

**27.** Rub the teeth with catechu-powder or with pure earth, so long as dental impurities are not removed.

दन्तमूलं परा धौतिर्योगिनां योगसाधने।
नित्यं कुर्य्यात्प्रभाते च दन्तरक्षां च योगवित्।
दन्तमूलं धावनादिकार्य्येषु योगिनां मतम्॥ २८॥

**28.** This teeth-washing is a great Dhauti and an important process in the practice of Yoga for the Yogīs. It should be done daily in the morning by the Yogīs, in order to preserve the teeth. In purification this is approved of by the Yogīs.

अथ जिह्वाशोधनम्

अथातः संप्रवक्ष्यामि जिह्वाशोधनकारणम्।
जरामरणरोगादीन्नाशयेद्दीर्घलम्बिका॥ २९॥

*(b²)* JIVHV ŚODHANA OR TONGUE-DHAUTI

**29.** I shall now tell you the method of cleansing the tongue. The elongation of the tongue destroys old age, death and disease.

अथ जिह्वामूलधौतिप्रयोगः

तर्जनीमध्यमानामा अङ्गुलित्रययोगतः।
वेशयेद्गलमध्ये तु मार्जयेल्लबिकामुलम्।
शनैः शनैर्मार्जयित्वा कफदोषं निवारयेत्॥ ३०॥

**30.** Join together the three fingers known as the index, the middle and the ring finger, put them into the throat, and rub well and clean the root of the tongue, and by washing it again throw out the phlegm.

मार्जयेन्नवनीतेन दोहयेच्च पुनः पुनः।
तदग्रं लौहयन्त्रेण कर्षयित्वा शनैः शनैः॥ ३१॥

**31.** Having thus washed it, rub it with butter; and milk it again and again; then by holding the tip of the tongue with an iron instrument pull it out slowly and slowly.

नित्यं कुर्य्यात्प्रयत्ने न रवेरुदयकेऽस्तके।
एवं कृते च नित्यं सा लम्बिका दीर्घतां व्रजेत्॥ ३२॥

**32.** Do this daily with diligence before the rising and setting sun. By so doing the tongue becomes elongated.

अथ कर्णधौतिप्रयोगः
तर्जन्यनामिकायोगान्मार्जयेत् कर्णरंध्रयोः।
नित्यमभ्यासयोगेन नादान्तरं प्रकाशयेत्॥ ३३॥

(*b*³) KARṆA-DHAUTI, OR EAR-CLEANING

**33.** Clean the two holes of the ears by the index and the ring fingers. By practising it daily, the mystical sounds are heard.

अथ कपालरन्ध्रप्रयोगः
वृद्धाङ्गुष्ठेन दक्षेण मार्जयेद्भालरन्ध्रकम्।
एवमभ्यासयोगेन कफदोषं निवारयेत्॥ ३४॥

KAPĀLA-RANDHRA-DHAUTI

**34.** Rub with the thumb of the right hand the depression in the forehead near the bridge of the nose. By the practice of this Yoga, diseases arising from derangements of phlegmatic humours are cured.

नाडी निर्मलतां याति दिव्यदृष्टिः प्रजायते।
निद्रान्ते भोजनान्ते च दिवान्ते च दिने दिने॥ ३५॥

**35.** The vessels become purified and clairvoyance is induced. This should be practised daily after awakening from sleep, after meals, and in the evening.

अथ हृद्धौतिः

हृद्धौतिं त्रिविधां कुर्य्याद्दण्डवमनवाससा॥ ३६॥

(c) HṚID-DHAUTI

**36.** Hṛd-Dhauti, or purification of heart (or rather throat) is of three kinds, *viz.*, by Daṇḍa (a stick), Vamana (vomiting), and by Vastra (cloth).

रम्भादडं हरिद्दडं वेत्रदण्डं तथैव च।
हृन्मध्ये चालयित्वा तु पुनः प्रत्याहरेच्छनैः॥ ३७॥

($c^1$) DAṆḌA-DHAUTI

**37.** Take either a plantain stalk or a stalk of turmeric (Haridrā) or a stalk of cane, and thrust it slowly into the aesophagus and then draw it out slowly.

कफपित्तं तथा क्लेदं रेचयेदूर्ध्ववर्त्मना।
दण्डधौतिविधानेन हृद्रोगं नाशयेद्ध्रुवम्॥ ३८॥

**38.** By this process all the phlegm, bile and other impurities are expelled out of the mouth. By this Daṇḍa-Dhauti every kind of heart disease is surely cured.

अथ वमनधौतिः

भोजनान्ते पिबद्वारि चाकण्ठपूरितं सुधीः।
उर्ध्वां दृष्टिं क्षणं कृत्वा तज्जलं वमयेत्पुनः।
नित्यमभ्यासयोगेन कफपित्तं निवारयेत्॥ ३९॥

($c^2$) VAMANA-DHAUTI

**39.** After meal, let the wise practitioner drink water full up to the throat, then looking for a short while upwards, let him vomit it out again. By daily practising this Yoga, disorders of phlegm and bile are cured.

अथ वासोधौतिः

चतुरङ्गुलविस्तारं सूक्ष्मवस्त्रं शनैर्ग्रसेत्।
पुनः प्रत्याहरेदेतत्प्रोच्यते धौतिकर्म्मकम्॥ ४०॥

(*c*³) VASTRA-DHAUTI

**40.** Let him swallow slowly a thin cloth, four fingers wide, then let him draw it out again. This is called Vastra-Dhauti.

गुल्मज्वरप्लीहाकुष्ठकफपित्तं विनश्यति।
आरोग्यं बलपुष्टिश्च भवेत्तस्य दिने दिने॥ ४१॥

**41.** This cures Gulma or abdominal diseases, fever, enlarged spleen, leprosy, and other skin diseases and disorders of phlegm and bile, and day by day the practitioner gets health, strength, and cheerfulness.

अथ मूलशोधनम्
अपानक्रूरता तापद्यावन्मूलं न शोधयेत्।
तस्मात्सर्वप्रयत्नेन मूलशोधनमाचरेत्॥ ४२॥

(*d*) MŪLA ŚODHANA, OR PURIFICATION OF THE RECTUM

**42.** The Apānavāyu does not flow freely so long as the rectum is not purified. Therefore with the greatest care let him practise this purification of the large intestines.

पित्तमूलस्य दण्डेन मध्यमाङ्गुलिनापि वा।
यत्नेन क्षालयेद्गुह्यं वारिणा च पुनः पुनः॥ ४३॥

**43.** By the stalk of the root of Haridrā (turmeric) or the middle finger, the rectum should be carefully cleansed with water over and over again.

वारयेत्कोष्ठकाठिन्यमामजीर्णं निवारयेत्।
कारणं कान्तिपुष्ट्योश्च वह्निमण्डल दीपनम्॥ ४४॥

**44.** This destroys constipation, indigestion, and dyspepsia, and increases the beauty and vigour of the body and enkindles the sphere of the fire (*i.e.*, the gastric juice).

*End of Dhautis*

---

## Part II

अथ बस्तिप्रकरणम्

जलबस्तिः शुष्कबस्तिर्बस्तिः स्याद्द्विविधा स्मृता।
जलबस्तिं जले कुर्याच्छुष्कबस्तिं सदा क्षितौ॥ ४५॥

BASTIS

**45.** The Bastis are described of two kinds, *viz*: Jala Basti (or water Basti) and Śuṣka Basti (or dry Basti). Water Basti is done in water and dry Basti always on land.

अथ जलबस्तिः

नाभिमग्नजले पायुं न्यस्तवानुत्कटासनम्।
आकुञ्चनं प्रसारञ्च जलबस्तिं समाचरेत्॥ ४६॥

JALA-BASTI

**46.** Entering water up to the navel and assuming the posture called Utkaṭāsana, let him contract and dilate the sphincter-muscle of the anus. This is called Jala-Basti.

प्रमेहञ्च उदावर्त्तं क्रूरवायुं निवारयेत्।
भवेत्स्वच्छन्ददेहश्च कामदेवसमो भवेत्॥ ४७॥

**47.** This cures Prameha (urinary disorders), udāvarta (disorders of digestion) and Krūravāyu (disorders of the wind). The body becomes free from all diseases and becomes as beautiful as that of the god Cupid.

बस्तिं पश्चिमोत्तानेन चालयित्वा शनैरधः।
अश्विनीमुद्रया पायुमाकुञ्चयेत् प्रसारयेत्॥ ४८॥

STHALA-BASTI

**48.** Assuming the posture called Paścimottāna, let him move the intestines slowly downwards, then contract and dilate the sphincter-muscle of the anus with Aśvini-Mudrā.

एवमभ्यासयोगेन कोष्ठदोषो न विद्यते।
विवर्द्धयेज्जठराग्निमामवातं विनाशयेत्॥ ४९॥

**49.** By this practice of Yoga, constipation never occurs, and it increases gastric fire and cures flatulence.

*End of Basti-Karma*

---

## Part III

अथ नेतियोगः
वितस्तिमानं सूक्ष्मसूत्रं नासानाले प्रवेशयेत्।
मुखान्निर्गमयेत्पश्चत् प्रोच्यते नेतिकर्मकम्॥ ५०॥

NETI

**50.** Take a thin thread, measuring half a cubit, and insert it into the nostrils, and passing it through, pull it out by the mouth. This is called Neti-Kriyā.

साधनान्नेतिकार्यस्य खेचरीसिद्धिमाप्नुयात्।
कफदोषा विनश्यन्ति दिव्यदृष्टिः प्रजायते॥ ५१॥

**51.** By practising the Neti-Kriyā, one obtains Khecarī Siddhi. It destroys the disorders of phlegm and produces clairvoyance or clear sight.

---

## Part IV

अथ लौकिकीयोगः
अमन्दवेगेन तुन्दं तु भ्रामयेदुभपार्श्वयोः॥
सर्वरोगान्निहन्तीह देहानलविवर्द्धनम्॥ ५२॥

LAUKIKĪ-YOGA

**52.** With great force move the stomach and intestines from one side to the other. This is called Laukikī-Yoga. This destroys all diseases and increases the bodily fire.

---

## PART V

**अथ त्राटकम्**

**निमेषोन्मेषकं त्यक्त्वा सूक्ष्मलक्ष्यं निरीक्षयेत्।**
**यावदश्रुन पतति त्राटकं प्रोच्यते बुधैः॥ ५३॥**

TRĀṬAKA OR GAZING

**53.** Gaze steadily without winking at any small object, until tears begin to flow. This is called Trāṭaka by the wise.

**एवमभ्यासयोगेन शाम्भवी जायते ध्रुवम्।**
**नेत्ररोगा विनश्यन्ति दिव्यदृष्टिः प्रजायते॥ ५४॥**

**54.** By practising this Yoga, Śāmbhavī Siddhis are obtained; and certainly all diseases of the eye are destroyed and clairvoyance is induced.

---

## PART VI

**अथ कपालभातिः**

**वामक्रमेणव्युत्क्रमेण शीत्क्रमेण विशेषतः।**
**भालभातिं त्रिधा कुर्यात्कफदोषं निवारयेत्॥ ५५॥**

KAPĀLABHĀTI

**55.** The Kapālabhāti is of three kinds : Vāma-krama, Vyūt-krama, and Śīta-krama. They destroy disorders of phlegm.

**अथ वामक्रमकपालभाति**

**ईडया पूरयेद्वायुं रेचयेत्पिङ्गलापुनः।**
**पिङ्गलया पूरयित्वा पुनश्चन्द्रेण रेचयेत्॥ ५६॥**

VĀMA-KRAMA

**56.** Draw the wind through the left nostril and expel it through the right, and draw it again through the right and expel it through the left.

पूरकं रेचकं कृत्वा वेगेन न तु चालयेत्।
एवमभ्यासयोगेन कफदोषं निवारयेत्॥ ५७॥

**57.** This inspiration and expiration must be done without any force. This practice destroys disorders of phlegm.

अथ व्युत्क्रमकपालभातिः

नासाभ्यां जलमाकृष्य पुनर्वक्त्रेण रेचयेत्।
पायं पायं व्युत्क्रमेण श्लेष्मदोषं निवारयेत्॥ ५८॥

VYUT-KRAMA

**58.** Draw the water through the two nostrils and expel it through the mouth slowly and slowly. This is called Vyut-krama which destroys disorders of phlegm.

अथ शीत्क्रमकपालभातिः

शीत्कृत्य पीत्वा वक्त्रेण नासानालैर्विरेचयेत्।
एवमभ्यासयोगेन कामदेवसमो भवेत्॥ ५९॥

ŚĪTA-KRAMA

**59.** Suck water through the. mouth and expel it through the nostrils. By this practice of Yoga one becomes like the god Cupid.

न जायते वार्द्धकं च ज्वरा नैव प्रजायते।
भवेत्स्वच्छन्ददेहश्च कफदोषं निवारयेत्॥ ६०॥

इति श्रीघेरण्डसंहितायां घेरण्डचण्डसंवादे षट्कर्म्मसाधनं नाम
प्रथमोपदेशः समाप्त॥ १॥

**60.** Old age never comes to him and decrepitude never disfigures him. The body becomes healthy, elastic, and disorders of phlegm are destroyed.

*End of the first lesson.*

---

# Lesson 2

## द्वितीयोपदेशः

### The Āsanas or Postures

**अथ आसनानि**

**घेरण्ड उवाच**

**आसनानि समस्तानि यावन्तो जीवजन्तवः।**
**चतुरशीतिलक्षाणि शिवेन कथितानि च॥ १॥**

GHERAṆḌA SAID

**1.** There are eighty-four hundreds of thousands of Āsanas described by Śiva. The postures are as many in number as there are numbers of species of living creatures in this universe.

**तेषां मध्ये विशिष्टानि षोडशोनं शतं कृतम्।**
**तेषां मध्ये मर्त्यलोके द्वात्रिंशदासनं शुभम्॥ २॥**

**2.** Among them eighty-four are the best; and among these eighty-four, thirty-two have been found useful for mankind in this world.

**अथ आसनानां भेदाः**

**सिद्धं पद्मं तथा भद्रं मुक्तं वज्रञ्च स्वस्तिकम्।**
**सिंहञ्च गोमुखं वीरं धनुरासनमेव च॥ ३॥**
**मृतं गुप्तं तथा मात्स्यं मत्स्येन्द्रासनमेव च।**
**गोरक्षं पश्चिमोत्तानं उत्कटं सङ्कटं तथा॥ ४॥**
**मयूरं कुक्कुटं कूर्म्मं तथा चोत्तानकुर्म्मकम्।**
**उत्तानमण्डुकं वृक्षं मण्डुकं गरुडं वृषम्॥ ५॥**

शलभं मकरं चोष्ट्रं भुजङ्गञ्चयोगासनम्।
द्वात्रिंशदासनानितु मर्त्त्यलोकेहि सिद्धिदम्।। ६।।

DIFFERENT KINDS OF POSTURES

**3–6.** The thirty-two Āsanas that give perfection in this mortal world are the follwing :—

1. Siddham *(Perfect posture)*.
2. Padmam *(Lotus posture)*.
3. Bhadram *(Gentle posture)*.
4. Muktam *(Free posture)*.
5. Vajram *(Adamant posture)*.
6. Svastika *(Prosperous posture)*.
7. Siṁham *(Lion posture)*.
8. Gomukha *(Cow-mouth posture)*.
9. Vīra *(Heroic posture)*.
10. Dhanur *(Bow posture)*.
11. Mṛtam *(Corpse posture)*.
12. Guptam (*Hidden posture)*.
13. Matsyam *(Fish posture)*.
14. Matsyendra.
15. Gorakṣa.
16. Paścimottāna.
17. Utkaṭam *(Hazardous posture)*.
18. Saṅkaṭam *( Dangerous posture)*.
19. Mayūram *(Peacock posture)*.
20. Kukkuṭam *(Cock posture)*.
21. Kūrma *(Tortoise posture)*.
22. Uttāna Maṇḍūka.
23. Uttāna Kūrmakam.
24. Vṛkṣa *(Tree posture)*.
25. Maṇḍūka *(Frog posture)*.
26. Garuḍa *(Eagle posture)*.
27. Vṛṣam *(Bull posture)*.
28. Śalabha *(Locust posture)*.
29. Makara *(Dolphin posture)*.
30. Uṣṭram *(Camel posture)*.
31. Bhujaṅgam *(Snake posture)*.
32. Yoga.

अथ आसनानां प्रयोगाः

अथ सिद्धासनम्

योनिस्थानकमङ्घ्रिमूलघटितं संपीड्य गुल्फेतरं
मेढ्रोपर्यंथ सन्निधाथ चिबुकं कृत्वा हृदि स्थापितम्।
स्थाणुः संयमितेन्द्रियोऽचलदृशा पश्यन् भ्रुवोरन्तर
मेवं मोक्षविधायतेफलकरं सिद्धासनं प्रोच्यते।। ७।।

1. THE SIDDHĀSANA

**7.** The practitioner who has subdued his passions, having placed one heel at the anal aperture should keep the other heel on the root of the generative organ; afterwards he should affix his chin upon the chest, and being quiet and straight, gaze at the spot between the two eye-brows. This is called the Siddhāsana and leads to emancipation.

अथ पद्मासनम्

वामोरूपरि दक्षिणां हि चरणां संस्थाप्य वामं तथा
दक्षोरूपरि पश्चिमेन विधिना कृत्वा कराभ्यां दृढम्।
अङ्गुष्ठौ हृदये निधाय चिबुकं नासाग्रमालोकये-
देतद्व्याधिविनाशनाशनकरं पद्मासनं प्रोच्यते।। ८।।

2. THE PADMĀSANA

**8.** Place the right foot on the left thigh and similarly the left one on the right thigh, also cross the hands behind the back and firmly catch hold of the great toes of feet so crossed. Place the chin on the chest and fix the gaze on the tip of the nose. This posture is called the Padmāsana (or Lotus posture). This posture destroys all diseases.

अथ भद्रासनम्

गुल्फौ च वृषणस्याधो यत्क्रमेण समाहितः।
पादाङ्गुष्ठौ कराभ्याञ्च धृत्वा च पृष्ठदेशतः।। ९।।

जालन्धरं समासाद्य नासाग्रमवलोकयेत्।
भद्रासनं भवेदेतत्सर्वव्याधिविनाशकम्॥ १०॥

3. THE BHADRĀSANA

**9–10.** Place the heels crosswise under the testes attentively; cross the hands behind the back and take hold of the toes of the feet. Fix the gaze on the tip of the nose, having previously adopted the Mudrā called Jālandhara. This is the Bhadrāsana (or happy posture) which destroys all sorts of diseases.

अथ मुक्तासनम्

पायुमूले वामगुल्फं दक्षगुल्फं तथोपरि।
समकायशिरोग्रीवं मुक्तासनन्तु सिद्धिदम्॥ ११॥

4. THE MUKTĀSANA

**11.** Place the left heel at the root of the organ of generation and the right heel above that, keep the head and the neck straight with the body. This posture is called the Muktāsana. It gives Siddhi (perfection).

अथ वज्रासनम्

जङ्घाभ्यां वज्रवत्कृत्वा गुदपार्श्वे पदावुभौ।
वज्रासनं भवेदेतद्योगिनां सिद्धिदायकम्॥ १२॥

5. THE VAJRĀSANA OR THE ADAMANT POSTURE

**12.** Make the thighs tight like adamant and place the legs by the two sides of the anus. This is called the Vajrāsana. It gives psychic powers to the Yogī.

अथ स्वस्तिकासनम्

जानूर्वोरन्तरे कृत्वा योगी पादतले उभे।
ऋजुकायः समासीनः स्वस्तिकं तत्प्रचक्षपते॥ १३॥

7. THE SWASTIKĀSANA

**13.** Drawing the legs and thighs together and

placing the feet underneath them, keeping the body in its easy condition and sitting straight, constitute the posture called the Svastikāsana.

अथ सिंहासनम्

गुल्फौ च वृषणस्याधो व्युत्क्रमेणोर्ध्वतां गतौ।
चितिमूलौ भूमिसंस्थौ कृत्वा च जानुनोपरि॥ १४॥
व्यक्तवक्त्रो जलंध्रञ्च नासाग्रमवलोकयेत्।
सिंहासनं भवेदेतत् सर्वव्याधिविनाशकम्॥ १५॥

7. THE SIṀHĀSANA

**14–15.** The two heels to be placed under the scrotum contrariwise (*i.e.*, left heel on the right side and the right heel on the left side of it) and turned upwards, the knees to be placed on the ground, (and the hands placed on the knees), mouth to be kept open; practising the Jālandhara mudrā one should fix his gaze on the tip of the nose. This is the Siṁhāsana (Lion-posture), the destroyer of all diseases.

अथ गोमुखासनम्

पादौ च भूमौ संस्थाप्य पृष्ठपार्श्वे निवेशयेत्।
स्थिरकायं समासाद्य गोमुखं गोमुखाकृति॥ १६॥

8. THE GOMUKHĀSANA

**16.** The two feet to be placed on the ground, and the heels to be placed contrariwise under the buttocks; the body to be kept steady and and the mouth raised, and sitting equably: this is called the Gomukhāsana: resembling the mouth of a cow.

अथ वीरासनम्

एकपादमथैकस्मिन्विन्यसेदूरुसंस्थितम्।
इतरस्मिंस्तथा पश्चाद्वीरासनमितीरितम्॥ १७॥

9. THE VĪRĀSANA

**17.** One leg (the right foot) to be placed on the other (left) thigh, and the other foot to be turned backwards : This is called the Vīrāsana (Hero-posture).

अथ धनुरासनम्

प्रसार्य्य पादौ भुवि दण्डरूपौ
करौ च पृष्ठे धृतपादयुग्मम्॥
कृत्वा धनुस्तुल्यपरिवर्त्तिताङ्गं
निगद्य योगी धनुरासनं तत्॥ १८॥

10. THE DHANURĀSANA

**18.** Spreading the legs on the ground, straight like a stick, and catching hold of (the toes of) the feet with the hands, and making the body bent like a bow, is called by the Yogīs the Dhanurāsana or Bow-posture.

अथ मृतासनम्

उत्तानं शववद्भूमौ शयानन्तु शवासनम्।
शवासनं श्रमहरं चित्तविश्रान्तिकारणम्॥ १९॥

11. THE MṚTĀSANA

**19.** Lying flat on the ground like a corpse is called the Mṛtāsana (the Corpse-posture). This posture destroys fatigue, and quiets the agitation of the mind.

अथ गुप्तासनम्

जानूर्वोरन्तरे पादौ कृत्वा पादौ च गोपयेत्।
पादोपरि च संस्थाप्य गुदं गुप्तासनं विदुः॥ २०॥

12. THE GUPTĀSANA

**20.** Hide the two feet under the two knees, and place the anus on the feet. This is known as the Guptāsana (Hidden-posture).

अथ मत्स्यासनम्

मुक्तपद्मासनं कृत्वा उत्तानशयनञ्चरेत्।
कूर्पराभ्यां शिरो वेष्ट्यं मत्स्यासनन्तु रोगहा॥ २१॥

13. THE MATSYĀSANA

**21.** Make the Padmāsana-posture (as stated in verse 8) without the crossing of the arms; lie on the back, holding the head by the two elbows. This is the Matsyāsana (Fish-posture), the destroyer of diseases.

अथ मत्स्येन्द्रासनम्

उदरं पश्चिमाभासं कृत्वा तिष्ठति यत्नतः।
नम्राङ्गं वामपादं हि दक्षजानूपरि न्यसेत्॥ २२॥
तत्र याम्यं कूर्परञ्च याम्यकरे च वक्त्रकम्।
भ्रुवोर्मध्ये गता दृष्टिः पीठं मात्स्येन्द्रमुच्यते॥ २३॥

14. THE MATSYENDARĀSANA

**22–23.** Keeping the abdominal region at ease like the back, bending the left leg, place it on the right thigh; then place on this the elbow of the right hand, and place the face on the palm of the right hand, and fix the gaze between the eye-brows. This is called the Matsyendra-posture.

अथ पश्चिमोत्तानासनम्

प्रसार्य पादौ भुवि दण्डरूपौ
संन्यस्तभालं चितियुग्ममध्ये।
यत्नेन पादौ च धृतौ कराभ्यां
योगीन्द्रपीठं पश्चिमोत्तानमाहुः॥ २४॥

15. THE PAŚCIMOTTĀNA-ĀSANA

**24.** Spread the two legs on the ground, stiff like a stick (the heels not touching), and place the forehead on the two knees, and catch with the hands the toes. This is called the Paścimottāna-Āsana.

अथ गोरक्षासनम्

जानूर्व्वोरन्तरे पादौ उत्तानौ व्यक्तसंस्थितौ।
गुल्फौ चाच्छाद्य हस्ताभ्यामुत्तानाभ्यां प्रयत्नतः॥ २५॥
कण्ठसंकोचनं कृत्वा नासाग्रमवलोकयेत्।
गोरक्षासनमित्याह योगिनां सिद्धिकारणम्॥ २६॥

16. THE GORAKṢĀSANA

**25–26.** Between the knees and the thighs, the two feet turned upward and placed in a hidden way, the heels being carefuny covered by the two hands outstretched; the throat being contracted, let one fix the gaze on the tip of the nose. This is called the Gorakṣāsana. It gives success to the Yogīs.

अथ उत्कटासनम्

अङ्गुष्ठाभ्यामवष्टभ्य धरां गुल्फौ च खे गतौ।
तत्रोपरि गुदं न्यस्य विज्ञेमुत्कटासनम्॥ २७॥

17. THE UTKAṬĀSANA

**27.** Let the toes touch the ground, and the heels be 'raised in the air; place the anus on the heels : this is known as the Utkaṭāsana.

अथ सङ्कटासनम्

वामपादं चितेर्मूलं संन्यस्य धरणीतले।
पाददण्डेन याम्यने वेष्टयेद्वामपादकम्।
जानुयुग्मे करयुग्ममेतत्सङ्कटमासनम्॥ २८॥

18. THE SAṄKAṬĀSANA

**28.** Placing the left foot and the leg on the ground, surround the left foot by the right leg; and place the two hands on the two knees. This is the Saṅkaṭāsana.

अथ मयूरासनम्

धरामवष्टभ्य करयोस्तलाभ्यां
तत्कूर्परे स्थापितनाभिपार्श्वम्।

उच्चासनो दण्डवदुत्थितः खे
मायूरमेतत्प्रवदन्ति पीठम्॥ २९॥
बहु कदशनभुक्तं भस्म कुर्यादशेषं
जनयतिजठराग्निं जारयेत्कालकूटम्।
हरति सकल रोगानाशु गुल्मज्वरादी-
न्भवति विगतदोषमासनं श्रीमयूरम्॥ ३०॥

19. THE MAYŪRĀSANA

**29–30.** Place the palms of the two hands on the ground, place the umbilical region on the two elbows, stand upon the hands, the legs being raised in the air, and crossed like Padmāsana. This is called the Mayūrāsana (Peacock-posture. The Peacock-posture destroys the effects of unwholesome food; it produces heat in the stomach; it destroys the effects of deadly poisons; it easily cures diseases, like Gulma and fever; such is this useful posture.

अथ कुक्कुटासनम्

पद्मासनं समासाद्य जानूर्वोरन्तरे करौ।
कर्पूराभ्यां समासीन उच्चस्थः कुक्कुटासनम्॥ ३१॥

20. THE KUKKUṬĀSANA

**31.** Sitting on the ground, cross the legs in the Padmāsana posture, thrust down the hands between the thighs and the knees, stand on the hands, supporting the body on the elbows. This is called the Cock-posture.

अथ कूर्मासनम्

गुल्फौ च वृषणस्याधो व्युत्क्रमेण समाहितौ।
ऋजुकायशिरोग्रीवं कूर्मासनमितीरितम्॥ ३२॥

21. THE KŪRMĀSANA

**32.** Place the heels contrariwise under the scrotum, stiffen (or keep at ease) the head, neck and body. This is called the Tortoise-posture.

अथ उत्तानकूर्मकासनम्

कुक्कुटासनबन्धस्थं कराभ्यां धृतकन्धरम्।
पीठं कूर्मवदुत्तानमेतदुत्तानकूर्मकम्॥ ३३॥

22. THE UTTĀNA KŪRMĀSANA

**33.** Assume the Cock-posture (as stated in verse 31), catch hold of the neck with the hands, and stand stretched like a tortoise. This is the Uttāna Kūrmāsana.

अथ मण्डूकासनम्

पादतलौ पृष्ठदेशे अङ्गुष्ठे द्वे च संस्पृशेत्।
जानुयुग्मं पुरस्कृत्य साधयेन्मण्डूकासनम्॥ ३४॥

23. THE MAṆḌŪKĀSANA

**34.** Carry the feet towards the back, the toes touching each other, and place the knees forwards. This is called the Frog-posture.

अथ उत्तानमण्डूकासनम्

माण्डूकासनमध्यस्थं कूर्पराभ्यां धृतं शिरः।
एतत् भेकवदुत्तानमेतदुत्तानमण्डुकम्॥ ३५॥

24. THE UTTĀNA MAṆḌŪKĀSANA

**35.** Assume the Frog-posture (as in verse 34), hold the head by the elbows, and stand up like a frog. This is called the Uttāna Maṇḍūkāsana.

अथ वृक्षासनम्

वामोरुमूलदेशे च याम्यं पादं निधाय तु।
तिष्ठेत्तु वृक्षवद्भूमौ वृक्षासनमिदं विदुः॥ ३६॥

25. THE VṚKṢĀSANA

**36.** Stand straight on one leg (the left), bending the right leg, and placing the right foot on the root of the left thigh; standing thus like a tree on the ground, is called the Tree-posture.

अथ गरुडासनम्

जङ्घोरुभ्यां धरां पीड्य स्थिरकायो द्विजानुना।
जानूपरि करयुग्मं गरुडासनमुच्यते॥ ३७॥

26. THE GARUḌĀSANA

**37.** Place the legs and the thighs on the ground pressing it, steady the body with the two knees, place the two hands on the knees : this is called the Garuḍa-posture.

अथ वृषासनम्

याम्यगुल्फे पायुमूलं वामभागे पदेतरम्।
विपरीतं स्पृशेद्भूमिं वृषासनमिदं भवेत्॥ ३८॥

27. THE VṚṢĀSANA

**38.** Place the anus on the right heel, on the left of it place the left leg crossing it opposite way, and touch the ground. This is called the Bull-posture.

अथ शलभासनम्

अध्यास्यः शेते करयुग्मं
वक्षेभूमिमवष्टभ्य करयोस्तलाभ्याम्।
पादौ च शून्ये च वितस्ति
चोर्ध्वं वदन्ति पीठं शलभं मुनीन्द्राः॥ ३९॥

28. THE ŚALABHĀSANA

**39.** Lie on the ground face downwards, the two hands being placed on the chest, touching the ground with the palms, raise the legs in the air one cubit high. This is called the Locust-posture.

अथ मकरासनम्

अध्यास्यः शेते हृदयं निधाय
भूमौ च पादौ च प्रसार्यमाणौ।
शिरश्च धृत्वा करदण्डयुग्मे-
देहाग्निकारं मकरासनं तत्॥ ४०॥

29. THE MAKARĀSANA

**40.** Lie on the ground face downwards, the chest touching the earth, the two legs being stretched : catch the head with the two arms. This is Makarāsana, the increaser of the bodily heat

अथ उष्ट्रासन

अध्यास्यः शते पदयुग्मव्यस्तं
पृष्ठे निधायापि धृतं कराभ्याम्॥
आकुञ्चयेत्सम्यगुदरास्यगाढ–
मौष्ट्रञ्च पीठं योगिनो वदन्ति॥ ४१॥

30. THE UṢṬRĀSANA

**41.** Lie on the ground face downwards, turn up the legs and place them towards the back, catch the legs with the hands, contract forcibly the mouth and the abdomen. This is called the Camel-posture.

अथ भुजङ्गासनम्

अङ्गुष्ठनाभिपर्यन्तमधोभूमौ विनिन्यसेत्।
करतलाभ्यां धरां धृत्वा ऊर्ध्वशीर्षः फणीव हि॥ ४२॥
देदाग्निर्वर्द्धते नित्यं सर्वरोगविनाशनम्।
जागर्ति भुजगी देवी भुजगासनसाधनात्॥ ४३॥

31. THE BHUJAṄGĀSANA

**42–43.** Let the body, from the navel downwards to the toes, touch the ground, place the palms on the ground, raise the head (the upper portion of the body) like a serpent. This is called the Serpent-posture. This always increases the bodily heat, destroys all diseases, and by the practice of this posture the serpent-Goddess (the kuṇḍalinī force) awakes.

अथ योगासनम्

उत्तानौ चरणौ कृत्वा संस्थाप्य जानुनोपरि।
आसनोपरि संस्थाप्य उत्तानं करयुग्मकम्॥ ४४॥
पूरकेर्वायुमाकृष्य नासाग्रमवलोकयेत्।
योगासनं भवेदेतद्योगिनां योगसाधने॥ ४५॥

इति श्रीघेरण्डसंहितायां घेरण्डचण्डसंवादे आसनप्रयोगो नाम
द्वितीयोपदेशः समाप्तः॥ २॥

32. THE YOGĀSANA

**44–45.** Turn the feet upwards, place them on the knees; then place the hands on the ground with the palms turned upwards; inspire, and fix the gaze on the tip of the nose. This is called the Yoga-posture, assumed by the Yogīs when practising Yoga.

———

## Lesson 3

# तृतीयोपदेशः

## On Mudrās

### अथ मुद्राकथनम्

घेरण्ड उवाच

महामुद्रा नभोमुद्रा उड्डीयानं जलन्धरम्।
मूलबन्धं महाबन्धं महावेधश्च खेचरी॥ १॥
विपरीतकरी योनिर्वज्रोली शक्तिचालनी।
ताडागी माण्डुकी मुद्रा शाम्भवी पञ्चधारणा॥ २॥
अश्विनी पाशिनी काकी मातङ्गी च भुजङ्गिनी॥
पञ्चविंशति मुद्राणि सिद्धदानीह योगिनाम्॥ ३॥

GHERAṆḌA SAID

**1–3.** There are twenty five mudrās, the practice of which gives success to the Yogīs. They are:— (1) Māhā-mudrā, (2) Nabho-mudrā, (3) Uḍḍīyāna, (4) Jālandhara, (5) Mūlabandha, (6) Mahābandba, (7) Mahāvedha, (8) Khecarī, (9) Viparītakarī, (10) Yoni, (11) Vajroṇī (12) Śakticālanī, (13) Taḍāgī, (14) Māṇḍavī, (15) Śāmbhavī, (16) Pañcadhāraṇā (five dhāraṇās), (21) Aśvinī, (22) Pāśinī, (23) Kākī, (24) Mātṅgī and (25) Bhujaṅginī.

### अथ मुद्राणां फलकथनम्

मुद्राणां पटलं देवि कथितं तव सन्निधौ।
येन विज्ञातमात्रेण सर्वसिद्धिः प्रजायते॥ ४॥
गोपनीयं प्रयत्नेन न देयं यस्य कस्यचित्।
प्रीतिदं योगिनाञ्चैव दुर्लभं मरुतामपि॥ ५॥

THE ADVANTAGES OF PRACTISING MUDRĀS

**4–5.** Maheśvara, when addressing his consort, has recited the advantages of Mudrās in these words : "O Devī! I have told you all the Mudrās; their knowledge leads to adeptship. It should be kept secret with great care, and should not be taught indiscriminately to every one. This gives happiness to the Yogīs, and is not to be easily attained by the ma-uts (gods of air) even."

अथ महामुद्राकथनम्

पायुमूलं वामगुल्फे संपीडा दृढयत्नतः।
याम्यपादं प्रसार्याथ करे धृतपदाङ्गुलः॥ ६॥
कण्ठसंकोचनं कृत्वा भ्रुवोर्मध्यं निरीक्षयेत्।
महामुद्राभिधा मुद्रा कथ्यते चैव सूरिभिः॥ ७॥

1. MAHĀ-MUDRĀ

**6–7.** Pressing carefully the anus by the left heel, stretch the right leg, and take hold of the great toe by the hand; contract the throat (not expelling the breath), and fix the gaze between the eye-brows. This is called Mahā-mudrā by the wise.

अथ महामुद्राफलकथनम्

क्षयकासं गुदावर्त्तं प्लीहापाणांर्ज्वीरं तथा।
नाशयेत्सर्वरोगाश्च महामुद्रा च साधनात्॥ ८॥

*Its benefits*

**8.** The practice of Mahā-mudrā cures consumption, the obstruction of the bowels, the enlargement of the spleen, indigestion and fever—in fact it cures all diseases.

अथ नभोमुद्राकथनम्

यत्र यत्र स्थितो योगी सर्वकार्येषु सर्वदा।
ऊर्ध्वजिह्वः स्थिरो भूत्वा धारयेत् पवनं सद॥
नभोमुद्रा भवेदेषा योगिनां रोगनाशिनी॥ ९॥

2. NABHOMUDRĀ

**9.** In whatever business a Yogī may be engaged, wherever he may be, let him always keep his tongue turned upwards (towards the soft palate), and restrain the breath. This is called Nabho-Mudrā; it destroys all the diseases of the Yogī.

अथ उड्डीयानबन्धः

उदरे पश्चिमं तानं नाभेरूर्ध्वं तु कारयेत्।
उड्डानं कुरुते यस्मादविश्रान्तं महाखगः।
उड्डीयानं त्वसौ बन्धो मृत्युमातङ्गकेसरी॥ १०॥

3. UḌḌĪYĀNĀ-BANDHA

**10.** Contract, the bowels equably above and below the navel towards the back, so that the abdominal viscera may touch the back. He who practises this Uḍḍīyāna (Flying up), without ceasing, conquers death. The Great Bird (Breath), by this process, is instantly forced up into the Suṣumnā, and flies (moves) constantly therein only.

अथ उड्डीयानबन्धस्य फलकथनम्

समग्राद्बन्धनाद् ध्र्येतदुड्डीयानं विशिष्यते।
उड्डीयने समभ्यस्ते मुक्तिः स्वाभाविकी भवेत्॥ ११॥

*Its benefits*

**11.** Of all Bandhanas, this is the best. The complete practice of this makes emancipation easy.

अथ जालन्धरबन्धकथनम्

कण्ठसंकोचनं कृत्वा चिबुकं हृदयेन्यसेत्।
जालन्धरे कृते बन्धे षोडशाधारबन्धनम्।
जालन्धरमहामुद्रा मृत्योश्च क्षयकारिणी॥ १२॥

4. JĀLANDHARA

**12.** Contracting the throat, place the chin on the chest. This is called Jālandhara. By this Bandha the sixteen Ādhāras are closed. This and the Mahāmudrā destroy death.

अथ जालन्धरबन्धस्य फलकथनम्

सिद्धं जालन्धरं बन्धं योगिनां सिद्धिदायकम्।
षण्मासमभ्यसेद्यो हि स सिद्धो नात्र संशयः॥ १३॥

*Its benefits*

**13.** The Jālandhara is a success-giving and well-tried Bandha; he who practises it for six months, becomes an adept without doubt.

अथ मूलबन्धकथनम्

पार्ष्णिना वामपादस्य योनिमाकुञ्चयेत्ततः।
नाभिग्रन्थिं मेरुदण्डे संपीड्य यत्नतः सुधीः॥ १४॥
मेढ्रं दक्षिणगुल्फे तु दृढबन्धं समाचरेत्।
जराविनाशिनी मुद्रा मूलबन्धो निगद्यते॥ १५॥

5. MŪLABANDHA

**14–15.** Press with the heel of the left foot the region between the anus and the scrotum, and contract the rectum; carefully press the intestines near the navel on the spine; and put the right heel on the organ of generation or pubes. This is called Mūlabandha, destroyer of decay.

अथ मूलबन्धस्य फलकथनम्।
संसारसमुद्रं तर्त्तुमभिलषति यः पुमान्।
विरले सुगुप्तो भूत्वा मुद्रामेतां समभ्यसेत्॥ १६॥
अभ्यासाद्बन्धनस्यास्य मरुत्सिद्धिर्भवेद् ध्रुवम्।
साधयेद् यत्नतो तर्हि मौनी तु विजितालसः॥ १७॥

*Its benefits*

**16–17.** The person who desires to cross the ocean of Existence, let him go to a retired place, and practise in secrecy this Mudrā. By the practice of it, the Vāyu (Prāṇa) is controlled undoubtedly; let one silently practise this, without laziness and with care.

अथ महाबन्धकथनम्
वामपादस्य गुल्फेन पायुमूलं निरोधयेत्।
दक्षपादेन तद्गुल्फं संपीड्य यत्नतः सुधीः॥ १८॥
शनैः शनैश्चालयेत् पार्ष्णिं योनिमाकुञ्चयेच्छनैः।
जालन्धरे धारयेत् प्राणं महाबन्धो निगद्यते॥ १९॥

6. MAHĀBANDHA

**18–19.** Close the anal orifice by the heel of the left foot, press that heel with the right foot carefully, move slowly and slowly the muscles of the rectum, and slowly contract the muscles of the yoni or perineum (space between anus and organ): restrain the breath by Jālandhara. This is called Mahābandha.

अथ महाबन्धस्य फलकथनम्
महाबन्धः परो बन्धो जरामरणनाशनः।
प्रसादादस्य बन्धस्या साधयेत् सर्ववाञ्छितम्॥ २०॥

*Its benefits*

**20.** The Mahābandha is the Greatest Bandha; it destroys decay and death: by virtue of this Bandha a man accomplishes all his desires.

अथ महावेधकथनम्

रूपयौवनलावण्यं नारीणां पुरुषं बिना।
मूलबन्धमहाबन्धौ महावेधं विना तथा॥ २१॥
महाबन्धं समासाद्य उड्डानकुम्भकं चरेत्।
महावेधः समाख्यातो योगिनां सिद्धिदायकः॥ २२॥

7. MAHĀVEDHA

**21–22.** As the beauty, youth and charms of women are in vain without men, so are Mūlabandha and Mahābandha without Mahāvedha. Sit first in Mahābandha posture, then restrain breath by Uḍḍāna Kumbhaka. This is called Mahāvedha—the giver of success to the Yogīs.

अथ महावेधस्य फलकथनम्

महाबन्धमूलबन्धौ महावेध समन्वितौ।
प्रत्यहं कुरुते यस्तु स योगी योगवित्तमः॥ २३॥
न मृत्युतो भयं तस्य न जरा तस्य विद्यते।
गोपनीयः प्रयत्नेन वेधोयं योगिपुङ्गवैः॥ २४॥

*Its benefits*

**23–24.** The Yogī who daily practises Mahābandha and Mūlabandha, accompanied with Mahāvedha, is the best of the Yogīs. For him there is no fear of death, and decay does not approach him: this Vedha should be kept carefully secret by the Yogīs.

अथ खेचरीमुद्राकथनम्

जिह्वाधो नाडीं संछिन्नां रसनां चालयेत् सदा।
दोहयेन्नवनीतेन लौहयन्त्रेण कर्षयेत्॥ २५॥

8. KHECARĪ MUDRĀ

**25.** Cut down the lower tendon of the tongue, *(frenulum linguae)* and move the tongue constantly : rub it with fresh butter, and draw it out (to lengthen it) with an iron instrument.

*N.B.*—This is the preliminary to Khecarī Mudrā. Its object is so to lengthen the tongue, that when drawn out it may touch with its tip the space between the eye-brows. This can be done by cutting away the lower tendon. It takes about three years to cut away the whole tendon. I saw my Guru doing it in this wise. On every Monday he used to cut the tendon one-twelfth of an inch deep and sprinkle salt over it, so that the cut portions might not join together. Then rubbing the tongue with butter he used to pull it out. Peculiar iron instruments are employed for this purpose; the painful process is repeated every week till the tongue can be stretched out to the requisite length.

**एवं नित्यं समभ्यासाल्लम्बिका दीर्घतां व्रजेत्।**
**यावद्गच्छेद् भ्रुवोर्मध्ये तदागच्छति खेचरी॥ २६॥**

**26.** By practising this always, the tongue becomes long, and when it reaches the space between the two eyebrows, then the Khecarī is accomplished.

**रसनां तालुमध्ये तु शनैः शनैः प्रवेशयेत्।**
**कपालकुहरे जिह्वा प्रपिविष्टा विपरीतगा।**
**भ्रुवोर्मध्ये गता दृष्टिर्मुद्रा भवति खेचरी॥ २७॥**

**27.** Then (the tongue being lengthened) practise, turning it upwards and backwards so as to touch the palate, till at length it reaches the holes of the nostrils opening into the mouth. Close those holes with the tongue (thus stopping inspiration), and fix the gaze on the space between the two eyebrows. This is called Khecarī.

**अथ खेचरी मुद्रायाः फलकथनम्**

**न च मूर्च्छा क्षुधा तृष्णा नैवालस्यं प्रजायते।**
**न च रोगो जरा मृत्युर्देवदेहः स जायते॥ २८॥**

*Its benefits*

**28.** By this practice there is neither fainting, nor hunger, nor thirst, nor laziness. There comes neither disease, nor decay, nor death. The body becomes divine.

**नाग्निना दह्यते गात्रं न शोषयति मारुतः।**
**न देहं क्लेदयन्त्यापो दंशयेन्न भुजङ्गमः॥ २९॥**

**29.** The body cannot be burned by fire, nor dried up by the air, nor wetted by water, nor bitten by snakes.

**लावण्यञ्च भवेद्गात्रे समाधिर्जायते ध्रुवम्।**
**कपालवक्त्रसंयोगे रसना रसमाप्नुयात्॥ ३०॥**

**30.** The body becomes beautiful; Samādhi is verily attained, and the tongue touching the holes obtains various juices (it drinks nectar).

**नानारससमुद्भूतमानन्दं च दिने दिने।**
**आदौ लवणक्षारञ्च ततस्तिक्तकषायकम्॥ ३१॥**
**नवनीतं घृतं क्षीरं दधि तक्रमधूनि च।**
**द्राक्षारसञ्च पीयूषं जायते रसनोदकम्॥ ३२॥**

**31–32.** Various juices being produced, day by day the experiences new sensations; first, he experiences a saltish taste, then alkaline, then bitter, then astringent, then he feels the taste of butter, then of ghee, then of milk, then of curd, then of whey, then of honey, then palm juice, and, lastly, arises the taste of nectar.

**अथ विपरीतकरणीमुद्राकथनम्**

**नाभिमूलेवसेत्सूर्यस्तालुमूले च चन्द्रमाः।**
**अमृतं ग्रस्ते सूर्यस्ततो मृत्युवशो नरः॥ ३३॥**
**ऊर्ध्वं च योजयेत् सूर्यञ्चन्द्रञ्च अध आनयेत्।**
**विपरीतकरी मुद्रासर्वतन्त्रेषु गोपिता॥ ३४॥**
**भूमौ शिरश्च संस्थाप्य करयुग्मं समाहितः।**
**उर्ध्वपादः स्थिरो भूत्वा विपरीतकरी मता॥ ३५॥**

9. VIVPARĪTAKARAṆĪ

**33–35.** The sun (the solar Nāḍī or plexus) dwells at the root of the navel, and the moon at the root of the palate; the process by which the sun is brought upward and the moon carried downward is called Viparītakaraṇī. It is a secret Mudrā in all the Tantras. Place the head on the ground, with hands spread, raise the legs up, and thus remain steady. This called Viparītakaraṇī.

**अथ विपरीतकरणीमुद्रायाः फलकथनम्**
**मुद्रां च साधयेन्नित्यं जरां मृत्युञ्च नाशयेत्।**
**स सिद्धः सर्वलोकेषु प्रलयेऽपि न सीदति॥ ३६॥**

*Its benefits*

**36.** By the constant practice of this Mudrā, decay and death are destroyed. He becomes an adept, and does not perish even at Pralaya.

**अथ योनिमुद्राकथनम्**
**सिद्धासनं समासाद्य कर्णचक्षुर्नसोमुखम्।**
**अङ्गुष्ठतर्जनीमध्यानामादिभिश्च साधयेत्॥ ३७॥**
**काकोभिः प्राणं संकृष्य अपाने योजयेत्ततः।**
**षट्चक्राणि क्रमाद्ध्यात्वा हुं हंसमनुना सुधीः॥ ३८॥**
**चैतन्यमानयेद्देवीं निद्रिता या भुजङ्गिनी।**
**जीवेन सहितां शक्तिं समुत्थाप्य कराम्बुजे॥ ३९॥**
**शक्तिमयः स्वयं भूत्वा परं शिवेन सङ्गमम्।**
**नानासुखं विहारञ्च चिन्तयेत् परमं सुखम्॥ ४०॥**
**शिवशक्तिसमायोगादेकान्तं भुवि भावयेत्।**
**आनन्दमानसो भूत्वा अहं ब्रह्मेति संभवेत्॥ ४१॥**
**योनिमुद्रा परा गोप्या देवानामपि दुर्ल्लभा।**
**सकृत्तु लाभसंसिद्धिः समाधिस्थः स एव हि॥ ४२॥**

10. YONIMUDRĀ

**37–42.** Sitting in Siddhāsana, close the two ears with the two thumbs, the eyes with the index fingers, the nostrils with the middle fingers, the upper lip with the fore fingers, and the lower lip with the little fingers. Draw in the Prāṇa-Vāyu by Kākī-mudrā, (as in verse 86) and join it with the Apāna-Vāyu; contemplating the six cakras in their order, let the wise one awaken the sleeping serpent-Goddess Kuṇḍalinī, by repeating the mantra Huṁ. (हुँ), and Haṁsa (हंसः), and raising the Śakti (Force-kuṇḍalī) with the jīva, place them at the thousand-petalled lotus. Being himself full of Śakti, being joined with the great Śiva, let him think of the various pleasures and enjoyments. Let him contemplate on the union of Śiva (spirit) and Śakti (Force or energy) in this world. Being himself all bliss, let him realise that he is the Brahma. This Yoni-mudrā is a great secret, difficult to be obtained even by the Devas. By once obtaining perfection in its practice, one enters verily into Samādhi.

**अथ योनिमुद्राफलकथनम्**

**ब्रह्महा भ्रूणहाचैव सुरापी गुरुतल्पगः।**
**एतैः पापैर्न लिप्येत योनिमुद्रानिबन्धनात्॥ ४३॥**
**यानि पापानि घोराणि उपपापानि यानि च।**
**तानि सर्वाणि नश्यन्ति योनिमुद्रानिबन्धनात्।**
**तस्मादभ्यसनं कुर्याद्यदि मुक्तिं समिच्छति॥ ४४॥**

*Its benefits*

**43–44.** By the practice of this Mudrā, one is never polluted by the sins of killing a Brāhmaṇa, killing a foetus, drinking liquor, or polluting the bed of the Preceptor. All the mortal sins and the venal sins are completely destroyed by the practice of this Mudrā. Let him therefore practise it, if he wishes for emancipation.

अथ वज्रोणीमुद्राकथनम्

धरामवष्टभ्य करयोस्तलाभ्यामूर्ध्वं क्षिपेत्पारयुगं शिरः खे।
शक्तिप्रबोधाय चिरजीवनाय वज्रोणीमुद्रां मुनयो वदन्ति॥ ४५॥

11. VAJROṆĪ MUDRĀ

**45.** Place the two palms on the ground, raise the legs in the air upward, the head not touching the earth. This awakens the Śakti, causes long life, and is called Vajroṇī by the sages.

अथ वज्रोणीमुद्रायाः फलकथनम्

अयं योगो योगश्रेष्ठो योगिनां मुक्तिकारणम्।
अयं हितप्रदो योगो योगिनां सिद्धिदायकः॥ ४६॥
एतद्योगप्रसादेन बिन्दुसिद्धिर्भवेद् ध्रुवम्।
सिद्धे बिन्दौ महायत्ने किं न सिद्ध्यतिभूतले॥ ४७॥
भोगेन महता युक्तो यदि मुद्रां समाचरेत्।
तथापि सकला सिद्धिस्तस्य भवति निश्चितम्॥ ४८॥

*Its benefits*

**46–48.** This practice is the highest of Yogas; it causes emancipation, and this beneficial Yoga gives perfection to the Yogīs. By virtue of this Yoga, the Bindu-Siddhi (retention of seed) is obtained, and when that Siddhi is obtained what else can he not attain in this world. Though immersed in manifold pleasures, if he practises this Mudrā, he attains verily all perfections.

अथ शक्तिचालनीमुद्राकथनम्

मूलाधारे आत्मशक्तिः कुण्डली परदेवता।
शयिता भुजगाकारा सार्द्धत्रिवलयान्विता॥ ४९॥

12. ŚAKTI CĀLANĪ

**49.** The great goddess Kuṇḍalinī, the energy of Self, ātma-śakti (spiritual force), sleeps in the Mūlādhāra (rectum); she has the form of a serpent having three coils and a half.

**यावत् सा निद्रिता देहे तावज्जीवः पशुर्यथा।**
**ज्ञानं न जायते तावत् कोटियोगं समभ्यसेत्॥ ५०॥**

**50.** So long as she is asleep in the body, the Jīva is a mere animal, and true knowledge does not arise, though he may practise ten millions of Yoga.

**उद्घाटयेत् कवाटञ्च यथा कुञ्चिकया हठात्।**
**कुण्डलिन्याः प्रबोधेन ब्रह्मद्वारं प्रभेदयेत्॥ ५१॥**

**51.** As by a key a door is opened, so by awakening the Kuṇḍalinī by Haṭha Yoga, the door of Brahma is unlocked.

**नाभिं संवेष्ट्य वस्त्रेण न च नग्नो बहिस्थितः।**
**गोपनीयगृहे स्थित्वा शक्ति चालनमभ्यसेत्॥ ५२॥**

**52.** Encircling the loins with a piece of cloth, seated in a secret room, not naked in an outer room, let him practise the Śakticālana.

**वितस्तिप्रमितं दीर्घं विस्तारे चतुरङ्गुलम्।**
**मृदुलं धवलं सूक्ष्मं वेष्टनाम्बरलक्षणम्।**
**एवमम्बरन्युक्तञ्च कटिसूत्रेण योजयेत्॥ ५३॥**

**53.** One cubit long, and four fingers (3 inches) wide, should be the encircling cloth, soft, white and of fine texture. Join this cloth with the Kaṭi-Sūtra (a string worn round the loins).

**भस्मना गात्रं संलिप्य सिद्धासनं समाचरेत्।**
**नासाभ्यां प्राणमाकृष्य अपाने योजयेद् बलात्॥ ५४॥**
**तावदाकुञ्चयेद्गुह्यं शनैश्विनीमुद्रया।**
**यावद्गच्छेत् सुषुम्नायां वायुः प्रकाशयेद्धठात्॥ ५५॥**

**54–55.** Rub the body with ashes, sit in Siddhāsana-posture, drawing the Prāṇa-Vāyu with the nostrils, forcibly join it with the Apāna. Contract the rectum slowly by the Aśvinī Mudrā, so long as the Vāyu does not enter the Suṣumnā, and manifests its presence.

तदा वायुप्रबन्धेन कुम्भिका च भुजङ्गिनी।
बद्धश्वासस्ततो भूत्वा ऊर्ध्वमार्गं प्रपद्यते॥ ५६॥

**56.** By restraining the breath by Kumbhaka in this way, the Serpent Kuṇḍalinī, feeling suffocated awakes and rises upwards to the Brahmarandhra.

विना शक्तिचालनेन योनिमुद्रा न सिद्ध्यति।
आदौ चालनमभ्यस्य योनिमुद्रां समभ्यसेत्॥ ५७॥

**57.** Without the Śākticālana, the Yoni-Mudrā is not complete or perfected; first the Cālana should be practised, and then the Yoni-Mudrā should be learnt.

इति ते कथितं चण्डकपाले शक्तिचालनम्।
गोपनीयं प्रयत्नेन दिने दिने समभ्यसेत्॥ ५८॥

**58.** O Caṇḍa-Kāpāli ! thus have I taught thee the Śakticālana. Preserve it with care : and practise it daily.

अथ शक्तिचालनीमुद्रायाः फलकथनम्

मुद्रेयं परमा गोप्या जरामरणनाशिनी।
तस्मादभ्यसनं कार्यं योगिभिः सिद्धिकाङ्क्षिभिः॥ ५९॥

*Its benefits*

**59.** This mudrā should be kept carefully concealed. It destroys decay and death. Therefore the Yogī, desirous of perfection, should practise it.

नित्यं योऽभ्यसते योगी सिद्धिस्तस्य करे स्थिता।
तस्य विग्रहसिद्धिः स्याद्रोगाणां संक्षयो भवेत्॥ ६०॥

**60.** The Yogī who practises this daily, acquires adeptship, attains Vigraha-siddhi and all his diseases are cured.

अथ तडागीमुद्राकथनम्

उदरं पश्चिमोत्तानं कृत्वा च तडागाकृति।
ताडागी सा परामुद्रा जरामृत्युविनाशिनी॥ ६१॥

13. TAḌĀGĪ-MUDRĀ

**61.** Sitting in Paścimottāna-posture, make the

stomach like a tank (hollow). This is Taḍāgī (Tank) Mudrā, destroyer of decay and death.

अथ माण्डुकीमुद्राकथनम्
मुखं समुद्रितं कृत्वा जिह्वामूलं प्रचालयेत्।
शनैर्ग्रसेदमृतं तन्माण्डुकीं मुद्रिकां विदुः॥ ६२॥

14. MĀṆḌUKI MUDRĀ

**62.** Closing the mouth, move the tip of the tongue towards the palate, and taste slowly the nectar (flowing from the Thousand-petalled Lotus). This is Frog-mudrā.

अथ माण्डुकीमुद्रायाः फलकथनम्
वलितं पलितं नैव जायते नित्ययौवनम्।
न केशे जायते पाको यः कुर्यान्नित्यमाण्डुकीम्॥ ६३॥

*Its benefits*

**63.** The body never sickens or becomes old, and it retains perpetual youth; the hair of him who practises this never grows white.

अथ शाम्भवीमुद्राकथनम्
नेत्राञ्जनं समालोक्य आत्मारामं निरीक्षयेत्।
सा भवेच्छाम्भवी मुद्रा सर्वतन्त्रेषु गोपिता॥ ६४॥

15. ŚĀMBHAVĪ MUDRĀ

**64.** Fixing the gaze between the two eye-brows, behold the Self existent. This is Śāmbhavī, secret in all the Tantras.

अथ शाम्भवीमुद्रायाः फलकथनम्
वेदशास्त्रपुराणानि सामान्यगणिका इव॥
इयं तु शाम्भवी मुद्रा गुप्ता कुलवधूरिव॥ ६५॥

*Its benefits*

**65.** The Vedas, the scriptures, the Purāṇas are like

public women, but this Śāmbhavī should be guarded as if it were a lady of a respectable family.

स एव आदिनाथश्च स च नारायणः स्वयम्।
स च ब्रह्मा सृष्टिकारी यो मुद्रां वेत्ति शाम्भवीम्॥ ६६॥

**66.** He, who knows this Śāmbhavī, is like the Ādinātha, he is a Nārāyaṇa, he is Brahmā the Creator.

सत्यं सत्यं पुनः सत्यं सत्यमुक्तं महेश्वर।
शाम्भवीं यो विजानीयात् स च ब्रह्म न चान्यथा॥ ६७॥

**67.** Maheśvara has said, "Truly, truly, and again truly, he who knows the Śambhavī, is Brahma. There is no doubt of this."

अथ पञ्चधारणामुद्राकथनम्

कथिता शाम्भवी मुद्रा शृणुष्व पञ्चधारणाम्।
धारणानि समासाद्य किं न सिध्यति भूतले॥ ६८॥

THE FIVE DHĀRAṆĀ-MUDRĀS

**68.** The Śambhavī has been explained; hear now the five Dhāraṇās. Learning these five Dhāraṇās, what cannot be accomplished in this world?

अनेन नरदेहेन स्वर्गेषु गमनागमम्।
मनोगतिर्भवेत्तस्य खेचरत्वं न चान्यथा॥ ६९॥

**69.** By this, with the human body one can visit and revisit Svarga-loka, he can go wherever he likes, as swiftly as mind, he acquires the faculty of walking in the sky. These five Dhāraṇās are :—Pārthivi (earthy), Āmbhasi (watery), Vāyavī (aerial), Āgneyī (fiery), and Ākāsī (ethereal).

अथ पार्थिवीधारणामुद्राकथनम्

यत्तत्त्वंह रितालदेशरचितं भौमं लकारान्वितं
वेदास्रं कमलासनेन सहितं कृत्वा हृदि स्थायिनम्।
प्राणं तत्र विलीय पञ्चघटिकाश्चित्तान्वितं धारये-
देषास्तम्भकरी सदा क्षितिजयं कुर्यादधोधारणा॥ ७०॥

*(a)* PĀRTHIVĪ

**70.** The Pṛthivī-Tattva has the colour of orpiment (yellow), the letter (la) **ल** is its secret symbol or seed (**बीज**), its form is four-sided, and Brahmā, its presiding deity. Place this Tattva in the heart, and fix by Kumbhakī the Prāṇa-Vāyus and the Citta there for the period of five ghaṭikās (2 hours). This is called Adhodhāraṇā. By this, one conquers the Earth, and no earthy-elements can injure him : and it causes steadiness.

**अथ पार्थिवीधारणामुद्रायाः फलकथनम्**

**पार्थिवीधारणामुद्रां यः करोति च नित्यशः।**
**मृत्युञ्जयः स्वयं सोपि स सिद्धो विचरेद् भुवि॥ ७१॥**

*Its benefits*

**71.** He who practises this dhāraṇā, becomes like the conqueror of Death; as an Adept he walks over this earth.

**अथ आम्भसीधारणामुद्राकथनम्**

**शङ्खेन्दुप्रतिमञ्च कुन्दधवलं तत्त्वं किलालं शुभं**
**तत्पीयूषवकारबीजसहितं युक्तं सदा विष्णुना।**
**प्राणं तत्र विलीय पञ्चघटिकाश्चित्तान्वितं धारयेदेषा**
**दुःसहतापपापहरणी स्यादाम्भसी धारणा॥ ७२॥**

*(b)* ĀMBHASĪ

**72.** The Water-Tattva is white like the Kunda-flower or a conch or the moon, its form is circular like the moon, the letter. **व** (va) is the seed of this ambrosial element, and Viṣṇu is its presiding deity. By Yoga, produce the water-tattva in the heart, and fix there the Prāṇa with the Citta (consciousness), for five ghaṭikās, practising Kumbhaka. This is Watery Dhāraṇā; it is the destroyer of all sorrows. Water cannot injure him who practises this.

अथ आम्भसीमुद्रायाः फलकथनम्
आम्भसीं परमां मुद्रां यो जानाति स योगवित्।
जले च गभीरे घोरे मरणं तस्य नो भवेत्।। ७३।।
इयं तु परमा मुद्रा गोपनीया प्रयत्नतः।
प्रकाशात् सिद्धिहानिः स्यात् सत्यं वच्मि च तत्त्वतः।। ७४।।

*Its benefits*

**73–74.** The Āmbhasī is a great mudrā; the Yogī who knows it, never meets death even in the deepest water. This should be kept carefully concealed. By revealing it success is lost, verily I tell you the truth.

अथ आग्नेयीधारणामुद्राकथनम्
यन्नाभिस्थितमिन्द्रगोपसदृशं बीजं त्रिकोणान्वितं
तत्त्वं तेजोमयं प्रदीप्तमरुणं रुद्रेण यत् सिद्धिदम्।
प्राणं तत्र विलीय पञ्चघटिकाश्चित्तान्वितं धारये-
देषा कालगभीरभीतिहरणी वैश्वानरी धारणा।। ७५।।

(*c*) ĀGNEYĪ

**75.** The Fire-Tattva is situated at the navel, its colour is red like the Indra-gôp insect, its form is triangular, its seed is (ra, र) its presiding deity is Rudra. It is refulgent like the sun, and the giver of success. Fix the Prāṇa along with the Citta in this Tattva for five ghaṭikās. This is called Fire-Dhāraṇā, destroyer of the fear of dreadful death, and fire cannot injure him.

अथ आग्नेयीधारणामुद्रायाः फलकथनम्
प्रदीप्ते ज्वलिते वह्नौ यदि पतति साधकः।
एतन्मुद्राप्रसादेन स जीवति न मृत्युभाक्।। ७६।।

*Its benefits*

**76.** If the practitioner is thrown into burning fire, by virtue of this Mudrā he remains alive, without fear of death.

अथ वायवीधारणामुद्राकथनम्

यद्भिन्नाञ्जनपुञ्जसन्निभमिदं धूम्रावभासं परं
तत्त्वं सत्त्वमयं यकारसहितं यत्रेश्वरो देवता।
प्राणं तत्र विलीय पञ्चघटिकाश्चित्तान्वितं धारयेदेषा
खे गमनं करोति यतिनां स्याद्वायवी धारणा॥ ७७॥

*(d)* VĀYAVĪ

**77.** The Air-tattva is black as unguent for the eyes (collirium), the letter य (ya) is its seed, and Īśvara its presiding deity. This Tattva is full of Satva quality. Fix the Prāṇa and the Citta for five ghaṭikās in this Tattva. This is Vāyavī-Dhāraṇā. By this, the practitioner walks in the air.

अथ वायवीधारणामुद्रायाः फलकथनम्

इयं तु परमा मुद्रा जरामृत्युविनाशिनी।
वायुना म्रियते नापि खे गतेश्च प्रदायिनी॥ ७८॥
शठाय भक्तिहीनाय न देया यस्य कस्यचित्।
दत्ते च सिद्धिहानिः स्यात् सत्यं वच्मि च चण्ड ते॥ ७९॥

*Its benefits*

**78–79.** This great Mudrā destroys decay and death. Its practitioner is never killed by any aerial disturbances; by its virtue one walks in the air. This should not be taught to the wicked or to those devoid of faith. By so doing success is lost; Oh Caṇḍa ! this is verily the truth.

अथ आकाशीधारणामुद्राकथनम्

यत् सिन्धौ वरशुद्धवारिसदृशं व्योमं परं भासितं
तत्त्वं देवसदाशिवेन सहितं बीजं हकारान्वितम्।
प्राणं तत्र विलीय पञ्चघटिकाश्चित्तान्वितं
धारयेदेषा मोक्षकवाटभेदनकरी कुर्यान्नभोधारणाम्॥ ८०॥

(*e*) ĀKĀŚĪ DHĀRAṆĀ

**80.** The Ether-Tattva has the colour of pure sea-water, **ह** (ha) is its seed, its presiding deity is Sadāśiva. Fix the Prāṇa along with Citta for five ghaṭikās in this Tattva. This is Ether-Dhāraṇā. It opens the gates of emancipation.

**अथ आकाशीधारणामुद्रायाः फलकथनम्।**
**आकाशीधारणां मुद्रां यो वेत्ति सच योगवित्।**
**न मृत्युर्जायते तस्य प्रलये नावसीदति।। ८१।।**

*Its benefits*

**81.** He who knows this Dhāraṇā is the real Yogī. Death does not approach him, nor does he perish at the Pralaya.

**अथ अश्विनीमुद्राकथनम्**
**आकुञ्चयेद् गुदद्वारं प्रकाशयेत् पुनः पुनः।**
**सा भवेदश्विनी मुद्रा शक्तिप्रबोधकारिणी।। ८२।।**

21. AŚVINĪ-MUDRĀ

**82.** Contract and dilate the anal aperture again and again, this is called Aśvinī-mudrā. It awakens the Śakti (Kuṇḍalinī).

**अश्विनीमुद्रायाः फलकथनम्**
**अश्विनी परमा मुद्रा गुह्यरोगविनाशिनी।**
**बलपुष्टिकरी चैव अकालमरणं हरेत्।। ८३।।**

*Its benefits*

**83.** This Aśvini is a great Mudrā; it destroys all diseases of the rectum; it gives strength and vigour, and prevents premature death.

**अथ पाशिनीमुद्राकथनम्**
**कण्ठपृष्ठे क्षिपेत् पादौ पाशवद् दढबन्धनम्।**

सा एव पाशिनी मुद्रा शक्ति प्रबोधकारिणी॥ ८४॥

22. PĀŚINĪ-MUDRĀ

**84.** Throw the two legs on the neck towards the back, holding them strongly together like a Pāśa (a noose). This is called Pāśinī-mudrā; it awakens the Śakti (Kuṇḍalinī.)

अथ पाशिनीमुद्रायाः फलकथनम्

पाशिनी महती मुद्रा बलपुष्टिविधायिनी।
साधनीया प्रयत्नेन साधकैः सिद्धिकाङ्क्षिभिः॥ ८५॥

*Its benefits*

**85.** This grand Mudrā gives strength and nourishment. It should be practised with care by those who desire success.

अथ काकीमुद्राकथनम्

काकचञ्चुवदास्येन पिबेद्वायुं शनैः शनैः।
काकीमुद्रा भवेद्देषा सर्वरोगविनाशिनी॥ ८६॥

23. KĀKĪ-MUDRĀ

**86.** Contract the lips, like the beak of a crow, and drink (draw in) the air slowly and slowly. This is Kākī (crow) mudrā, destroyer of all diseases.

अथ काकीमुद्रायाः फलकथनम्

काकीमुद्रा परा मुद्रा सर्वतन्त्रेषु गोपिता।
अस्याः प्रसादमात्रेण न रोगी काकवद् भवेत्॥ ८७॥

*Its benefits*

**87.** The Kākī Mudrā is a great Mudrā, kept secret in all Tantras. By virtue of this, one becomes free from disease like a crow.

अथ मातङ्गिनीमुद्राकथनम्

कण्ठमग्ने जले स्थित्वा नासाभ्यां जलमाहरेत्।

मुखान्निर्गमयेत् पश्चात् पुनर्वक्त्रेण चाहरेत्॥ ८८॥
नासाभ्यां रेचयेत् पश्चात् कुर्यादेवं पुनः पुनः।
मातङ्गिनी परा मुद्रा जरामृत्युविनाशिनी॥ ८९॥

24. MĀTAṄGINĪ-MUDRĀ

**88–89.** Stand in neck-deep water, draw in the water through the nostrils, and throw it out by the mouth. Then draw in the water through [the mouth and expel it through] the nostrils. Let one repeat this again and again. This is called Elephant-mudrā, destroyer of decay and death.

अथ मातङ्गिनीमुद्रायाः फलकथनम्
विरले निर्जने देशे स्थित्वा चैकाग्रमानसः।
कुर्यान्मातङ्गिनीं मुद्रां मातङ्ग इव जायते॥ ९०॥
यत्र यत्र स्थितोयोगी सुखमत्यन्तमश्नुते।
तस्मात् सर्वप्रयत्नेन साधयेन्मुद्रिकां पराम्॥ ९१॥

*Its benefits*

**90–91.** In a solitary place, free from human intrusion, one should practise with fixed attention this Elephant mudrā : by so doing, he becomes strong like Elephant. Wherever he may be, by this process the Yogī enjoys great pleasure; therefore this mudrā should be practised with great care.

अथ भुजङ्गिनीमुद्राकथनम्
वक्त्रं किञ्चित् सुप्रसार्य चानिलं गलया पिबेत्।
सा भवेद् भुजगी मुद्रा जरामृत्युविनाशिनी॥ ९२॥

25. BHUJAṄGINĪ MUDRĀ

**92.** Extending the neck a little forward, let him drink (draw in) air through the aesophagus; this is called Serpent-mudrā, destroyer of decay and death.

अथ भुजङ्गिनीमुद्रायाः फलकथनम्

यावच्च उदरे रोगा अजीर्णादि विशेषतः।
तत् सर्वं नाशयेदाशु यत्र मुद्रा भुजङ्गिनी॥ ९३॥

*Its benefits*

**93.** This Serpent-mudrā quickly destroys all stomach diseases, especially indigestion, dyspepsia, etc.

अथ मुद्राणां फल कथनम्

इदं तु मुद्रापटलं कथितं चण्ड ते शुभम्।
वल्लभं सर्वसिद्धानां जरामरणनाशनम्॥ ९४॥

THE BENEFITS OF MUDRĀS

**94.** O Caṇḍa-Kāpāli! thus have I recited to thee the chapter on Mudrās. This is beloved of all adepts, and destroys decay and death.

शठाय भक्तिहीनाय न देयं यस्य कस्यचित्।
गोपनीयं प्रयत्नेन दुर्लभं मरुतामपि॥ ९५॥

**95.** This should not be taught indiscriminately, nor to a wicked person, nor to one devoid of faith; this should be preserved secret with great care; it is difficult to be attained even by the Devas.

ऋजवे शान्तचिताय गुरुभक्तिपराय च।
कुलीनाय प्रदातव्यं भोगमुक्तिप्रदायकम्॥ ९६॥

**96.** These Mudrās which give happiness and emancipation should be taught to a guileless, calm and peace-minded person, who is devoted to his Teacher and comes of good family.

मुद्राणां पटलं ह्येतत् सर्वव्याधिविनाशनम्।
नित्यमभ्यासशीलस्य जठराग्निविवर्धनम्॥ ९७॥

**97.** These Mudrās destroy all diseases. They increase the gastric fire of him who practises them daily.

न तस्य जायते मृत्युर्नास्य जरादिकं तथा।
नाग्निजलभयं तस्य वायोरपि कुतो भयम्॥ ९८॥

**98.** To him death never comes, nor decay, etc.; there is no fear to him from fire and water, nor from air.

कासः श्वासः प्लीहा कुष्ठं श्लेष्मरोगाश्च विंशतिः।
मुद्राणां साधनाच्चेव विनश्यन्ति न संशयः॥ ९९॥

**99.** Cough, asthma, enlargement of spleen, leprosy, being diseases of twenty sorts, are verily destroyed by the practice of these Mudrās.

बहुना किमिहोक्तेन सारं वच्मि च चण्ड ते।
नास्ति मुद्रासमं किञ्चित् सिद्धिदं क्षितिमण्डले॥ १००॥

इति श्रीघेरण्डसंहितायां घेरण्डचण्डसंवादे घटस्थयोगप्रकरणे मुद्राप्रयोगो नाम तृतीयोपदेशः॥

**100.** O Caṇḍa! What more shall I tell thee? In short, there is nothing in this world like the Mudrās for giving quick success.

---

# Lesson 4

## चतुर्थोपदेशः

## Pratyāhāra, or Restraining the Mind

घेरण्ड उवाच
अथातः संप्रवक्ष्यामि प्रत्याहारकमुत्तमम्।
यस्य विज्ञानमात्रेण कामादिरिपुनाशनम्॥ १॥

GHERAṆḌA SAID

**1.** Now I shall tell thee, Pratyāhāra-Yoga the best. By its knowledge, all the passions like lust, etc., are destroyed.

यतो यतो निश्चरति मनश्चञ्चलमस्थिरम्।
ततस्ततो नियम्यैतदात्मन्येव वशं नयेत्॥ २॥

**2.** Let one bring the Citta (thinking principle) under his control by withdrawing it, whenever it wanders away drawn by the various objects of sight.

पुरस्कारं तिरस्कारं सुश्राव्यं वा भयानकम्।
मनस्तस्मान्नियम्यैतदात्मन्येव वशं नयेत्॥ ३॥

**3.** Praise or censure; good speech or bad speech; let one withdraw his mind from all these and bring the Citta under the control of the Self.

सुगन्धे वापि दुर्गन्धे घ्राणेषु जायते मनः।
तस्मात् प्रत्याहरेदेतदात्मन्येव वशं नयेत्॥ ४॥

**4.** From sweet smells or bad smells, by whatever odour the mind may be distracted or attracted, let one withdraw the mind from that, and bring the thinking principle under the control of his Self.

मधुराम्लकतिक्तादिरसं गतं यदा मनः।
तस्मात् प्रत्याहरेदेतदात्मन्येव वशं नयेत्॥ ५॥
इति श्रीघेरण्डसंहितायां घेरण्डचण्डसंवादे घटस्थयोगे
प्रत्याहारप्रयोगो नाम चतुर्थोपदेशः।

**5.** From sweet or acid tastes, from bitter or astringent tastes, by whatever taste the mind may be attracted, let one withdraw it from that, and bring it within the control of his Self.

---

# Lesson 5

## पञ्चमोपदेशः

## Prāṇāyāma, or Restraint of Breath

**घेरण्ड उवाच**

**अथातः संप्रवक्ष्यामि प्राणायामस्य यद्विधिम्।**
**यस्य साधनमात्रेण देवतुल्यो भवेन्नरः॥ १॥**

GHERAṆḌA SAID

**1.** Now I shall tell thee the rules of Prāṇāyāma or regulation of breath. By its practice a man becomes like a god.

**आदौ स्थानं तथा कालं मिताहारं तथापरम्।**
**नाडीशुद्धिं ततः पश्चात् प्राणायामं च साधयेत्॥ २॥**

**2.** Four things are necessary in practising Prāṇāyāma. First, a good place; second, a suitable time; third, moderate food; and, lastly, the purifications of the nāḍīs, (vessels of the body, *i.e.*, alimentary canal, etc.).

**अथ स्थाननिर्णयः**

**दूरदेशे तथारण्ये राजधान्यां जनान्तिके।**
**योगारम्भं न कुर्वीत कृतश्चेत् सिद्धिहा भवेत्॥ ३॥**

*Place*

**3.** The practice of Yoga should not be attempted in a far off country (from home), nor in a forest, nor in a capital city, nor in the midst of a crowd. If one does so, he loses success.

अविश्वासं दूरदेशे अरण्ये रक्षिवर्जितम्।।
लोकारण्ये प्रकाशश्च तस्मात् त्रीणि विवर्जयेत्।। ४।।

**4.** In a distant country, one loses faith (because of the Yoga not being known there); in a forest, one is without protection; and in the midst of a thick population, there is danger of exposure (for then the curious will trouble him). Therefore, let one avoid these three.

सुदेशे धार्मिके राज्ये सुभिक्षे निरुपद्रवे।
तत्रैकं कुटीरं कृत्वा प्राचीरैः परिवेष्टितम्।। ५।।

**5.** In a good country whose king is just, where food is easily and abundantly procurable, where there are no disturbances, let one erect there a small hut, around it let him raise walls.

वापीकूपतडागं च प्राचीरमध्यवर्ति च।
नात्युच्चं नातिनिम्नं च कुटीरं कीटवर्जितम्।। ६।।

**6.** And in the centre of the enclosure, let him sink a well and dig a tank. Let the hut be neither very high nor very low : let it be free from insects.

सम्यग्गोमयलिप्तं च कुटीरन्तत्रनिर्मितं।
एवं स्थानेषु गुप्तेषु प्राणायामं समभ्यसेत्।। ७।।

**7.** It should be completely plastered over with cow-dung. In a hut thus built and situated in such a hidden place, let him practise Prāṇāyāma.

अथ कालनिर्णयः

हेमन्ते शिशिरे ग्रीष्मे वर्षायां च ऋतौ तथा।
योगारम्भं न कुर्वीत कृते योगो हि रोगदः।। ८।।

*Time*

**8.** The practice of Yoga should not be commenced in these four seasons out of six :—hemanta (winter), śiśira (cold), grīṣma (hot), varṣā (rainy). If one begins in these seasons, one will contract diseases.

**वसन्ते शरदि प्रोक्तं योगारम्भं समाचरेत्।**
**तथायोगी भवेत् सिद्धो रोगान्मुक्तो भवेद् ध्रुवम्॥ ९॥**

**9.** The practice of Yoga should be commenced by a beginner in spring (vasanta); and autumn (śarat). By so doing, he attains success; and verily he does not become liable to diseases.

**चैत्रादिफाल्गुनान्ते च माघादिफाल्गुनान्तिके।**
**द्वौ द्वौ मासौ ऋतुभागौ अनुभावश्चतु श्चतुः॥ १०॥**

**10.** The six seasons occur in their order in the twelve months beginning with Caitra and ending with Phālguna: two months being occupied by each season. But each season is experienced for four months, beginning with Māgha and ending with Phālguna.

**वसन्तश्चैत्र वैशाखौ ज्येष्ठाषाढा च ग्रीष्मकौ।**
**वर्षा श्रावणभाद्राभ्यां शरदाश्विनकार्तिकौ।**
**मार्गपौषौ च हेमन्तः शिशिरो माघफाल्गुनौ॥ ११॥**

SIX SEASONS

**11.** The Six seasons are as follows :—

| *Season* | *Months (Sanskrit)* | *English* |
|---|---|---|
| Vasanta or Spring | Caitra and Vaiśākha | March, April |
| Grīṣma or Summer | Jyeṣṭha and Āṣāḍha | May, June |
| Varṣā or Rainy | Śrāvaṇa and Bhādra | July, August |
| Śarat or Autumn | Āśvina and Kārtika | Sept., Oct. |
| Hemanta or Winter | Agrahāyaṇa and Pauṣa | Nov., Dec. |
| Śiśira or Cold | Māgha and Phālguna | Jan., Feb. |

**अनुभावं प्रवक्ष्यामि ऋतूनां च यथोदितम्।**
**माघादिमाधवान्तेषु वसन्तानुभवं विदुः॥ १२॥**
**चैत्रादि चाषाढातं च निदाघानुभवं विदुः।**
**आषाढादि चाश्विनान्तं प्रावृषानुभवं विदुः॥ १३॥**
**भाद्रादिमार्गशीर्षान्तं शरदोऽनुभवं विदुः।**
**कार्तिकादिमाघमासान्तं हेमन्तानुभवं विदुः।**
**मार्गादिचतुरो मासाञ्च शिशिरानुभवं विदुः॥ १४॥**

*The experiencing of seasons*

**12–14.** Now I shall tell thee the experiencing of seasons. They are as follows :—

| *Beginning from* | *Ending with* | *Seasons* | *English* |
|---|---|---|---|
| Māgha | Vaiśākha | Varṣānubhava | Jan. to April. |
| Caitra | Āṣāḍha | Grīṣmānubhava | March to June. |
| Āṣāḍha | Āśvina | Varṣānubhava | June to Sept. |
| Bhādra | Agrahāyaṇa | Śradānubhava | August to Nov. |
| Kārtika | Māgha | Hemantānubhava | Oct. to Jan. |
| Agrahāyaṇa | Phālguna | Śiśirānubhava | Nov. to Feb. |

**वसन्ते वापि शरदि योगारम्भं समाचरेत्।**
**तदा योगो भवेत् सिद्धोविनायासेन कथ्यते॥ १५॥**

**15.** The practice of Yoga should be commenced either in Vasanta (spring) or Śarat (autumn). For in these seasons success is attained without much trouble.

**अथ मिताहारः**

**मिताहारं विना यस्तु योगारम्भं तु कारयेत्।**
**नानारोगो भवेत्तस्य किञ्चिद्योगो न सिध्यति॥ १६॥**

*Moderation of diet*

**16.** He who practises Yoga without moderation of diet, incurs various diseases, and obtains no success.

**शाल्यन्नं यवपिष्ठं वा गोधूमपिष्टकं तथा।**
**मुद्म्भाषचणकादि शुभ्रं च तुषवर्जितम्॥ १७॥**

**17.** A Yogī should eat rice, barley (bread), or wheaten bread. He may eat Mudga beans (Phaseolus Mungo), Māṣa beans (Phaseolus Radiatus), gram, etc. These should be clean, white and free from chaff.

**पटोलं पनसं मानं कक्कोलं च शुकाशकम्।**
**द्राढिकां कर्कटीं रम्भां डुम्बरीं कण्टकण्टकम्॥ १८॥**
**आमरम्मां भालरम्भां रम्भादण्डं च मूलकम्।**
**वार्ताकीं मूलकं ऋद्धिंयोगी भक्षणमाचरेत्॥ १९॥**

**18–19.** A Yogī may eat paṭola (a kind of cucumber,**परवर**), jackfruit, mānakachu (Arum Colocasia), kakkola (a kind of berry), the jujube, the bonduc nut (Bonducella guilandina), cucumber, plantain, fig; the unripe plantain, the small plantain, the plantain stem, and roots, brinjal, and medicinal roots and fruits (*e.g.*, ṛddhi, etc.)

**बालशाकं कालशाकं तथा पटोलपत्रकम्।**
**पञ्चशाकं प्रशंसीयाद्वास्तूकं दिलमोचिकाम्।। २०।।**

**20.** He may eat green, fresh vegetables **बालशाक,** black vegetables (**कालशाक**), the leaves of paṭola, the Vāstūka-śāka, and hima-locikā Śāka. These are the five śākas (vegetable leaves) praised as fit food for Yogīs.

**शुद्धं सुमधुरं स्निग्धं उदरार्धविवर्जितम्।**
**भुज्यते सुरसं प्रीत्या मिताहारमिमं विदुः।। २१।।**

**21.** Pure, sweet and cooling food should be eaten to fill half the stomach: eating thus sweet juices with pleasure, and leaving the other half of the stomach empty is called moderation in diet.

**अन्नेन पूरयेदर्धं तोयेन तु तृतीयकम्।**
**उदरस्य तुरीयांशं संरक्षेद्वायुचारणे।। २२।।**

**22.** Half the stomach should be filled with food, one quarter with water: and one quarter should be kept empty for practising prāṇāyāma.

**कट्वल्मं लवणं तिक्तं भृष्टं च दधि तक्रकम्।**
**शाकोत्कटं तथा मद्यं तालं च पनसं तथा।। २३।।**

*Prohibited foods*

**23.** In the beginning of Yoga-practice one should discard bitter, acid, salt, pungent and roasted things, curd, whey, heavy vegetables, wine, palmnuts, and over-ripe jack-fruit.

कुलत्थं मसूरं पाण्डुं कूष्माण्डं शाकदण्डकम्।
तुम्बीकोलकपित्थं च कण्टबिल्वं पलाशकम्।। २४।।

**24.** So also kulattha and masur beans, pāṇḍu fruit, pumpkins and vegetable stems, gourds, berres, kaṭhabel, (feronia elephantum), kaṇṭabilva and palāśa (Butea frondosa).

कदम्बं जम्बीरं बिम्बं लकुचं लशुनं विषम्।
कामरङ्गं पियालं च हिंगुशाल्मलीकेमुकम्।। २५।।

**25.** So also Kadamba (Nauclea cadamba), jambīra (citron), bimba, lukuca (a kind of bread fruit tree), onions, lotus, kāmaraṅga, piyāla (Buchanānia latifolia), hiṅga (assafoetida), śālmali, kemuka.

योगारम्भे वर्जयेच्च पथस्त्रीवह्निसेवनम्।
नवनीतं घृतं क्षीरं गुडं शर्करादि चैक्षवम्।। २६।।
पक्करम्भां नारिकेलं दाडिम्बमशिवासवम्।
द्राक्षाङ्गुलवनीं धात्रीं रसमाम्लावविर्जितम्।। २७।।

**26–27.** A beginner should avoid much travelling, company of women, and warming himself by fire. So also he should avoid fresh butter, ghee, thickened milk, sugar, and date-sugar, etc., as well as ripe plantain, cocoa-nut, pomegranate, dates, lavanī fruit, āmlaki (myrobalans), and everything containing acid juices.

एलाजातिलवङ्गं च पौरुषं जम्बु जाम्बलम्।
हरीतकीं खर्जूरं च योगी भक्षणमाचरेत्।। २८।।

**28.** But cardamom, jaiphal, cloves, aphrodisiacs or stimulants, the rose-apple, harītaki, and palm dates, a Yogī may eat while practising Yoga.

लघुपाकं प्रियं स्निग्धं तथा धातुप्रपोषणम्।
मनोऽभिलषितं योग्यं योगी भोजनमाचरेत्।। २९।।

**29.** Easily digestible, agreeable and cooling foods which nourish the humours of the body, a Yogī may eat according to his desire.

**काठिन्यं दुरितं पूतिमुष्णं पर्युषितं तथा।**
**अतिशीतं चातिचोष्णं भक्ष्यं योगी विवर्जयेत्॥ ३०॥**

**30.** But a Yogī should avoid hard (not easily digestible), sinful food, or putrid food, or very hot, or very stale food, as well as very cooling or very much exciting food.

**प्रातःस्नानोपवासादि कायक्लेशविधिं तथा।**
**एकाहारं निराहारं यामान्ते च न कारयेत्॥ ३१॥**

**31.** He should avoid early (morning before sun-rise) baths, fasting, etc., or anything giving pain to the body; so also is prohibited to him eating only once a day, or not eating at all. But he may remain without food for 3 hours.

**एवं विधिविधानेन प्रणायामं समाचरेत्।**
**आरम्भे प्रथमे कुर्यात् क्षीराज्यं नित्यभोजनम्।**
**मध्याह्ने चैव सायाह्ने भोजनद्वयमाचरेत्॥ ३२॥**

**32.** Regulating his life in this way, let him practise Prāṇāyāma. In the beginning before commencing it, he should take a little milk and ghee daily, and take his food twice daily, once at noon, and once in the evening.

**इति मिताहारः।**

---

**अथ नाडीशुद्धिः**

**कुशासने मृगाजिने व्याघ्राजिने च कम्बले।**
**स्थलासने समासीनः प्राङ्मुखो वाप्युदङ्मुखः।**
**नाडीशुद्धिं समासाद्य प्राणायाम समभ्यसेत्॥ ३३॥**

PURIFICATION OF NĀḌĪS.

**33.** He should sit on a seat of Kuśa-grass, or an antelope skin, or tiger skin or a blanket, or on earth, calmly and quietly, facing east or north. Having purified the nāḍīs, let him begin Prāṇāyāma.

चण्डकापालिरुवाच
नाडीशुद्धिं कथं कुर्यान्नाडीशुद्धिस्तु कीदृशी।
तत् सर्वं श्रोतुमिच्छामि तद्वदस्व दयानिधे॥ ३४॥

CANḌAKĀPĀLI SAID

**34.** O ocean of mercy! How are nāḍīs purified, what is the purification of nāḍīs; I want to learn all this; recite this to me.

घेरण्ड उवाच
मलाकुलासु नाडीषु मारुतो नैव गच्छति।
प्राणायामः कथं सिध्येत्तत्त्वज्ञानं कथं भवेत्।
तस्मादादौ नाडीशुद्धिं प्राणायामं ततोऽभ्यसेत्॥ ३५॥

GHERAṆḌA SAID

**35.** The Vāyu does not (cannot) enter the nāḍīs so long as they are full of impurities (*e.g.*, faeces, etc.). How then can Prāṇāyāma be accomplished? How can there be knowledge of Tattvas? Therefore, first the Nāḍīs should be purified, and then Prāṇāyāma should be practised.

नाडीशुद्धिर्द्विधा प्राक्ता समनुर्निर्मनुतथा।
बीजेन समनुं कुर्यान्निर्मुनुं धौतकर्मणा॥ ३६॥

**36.** The purification of nāḍīs is of two sorts :— Samanu and Nirmanu. The Samanu is done by a mental process with Bīja-mantra. The Nirmanu is performed by physical cleanings.

धौतकर्म पुरा प्रोक्तं षट्कर्मसाधने यथा।
शृणुष्व समनुं चण्ड नाडीशुद्धिर्यथा भवेत्॥ ३७॥

**37.** The physical cleanings or Dhautis have already been taught. They consist of the six Sādhanas. Now, O Caṇḍa, listen to the Samanu process of purifying the vessels.

उपविश्यासने योगी पद्मासनं समाचरेत्।
गुर्वादिन्यासनं कुर्याद् यथैव गुरुभाषितम्।
नाडीशुद्धिं प्रकुर्वीत प्राणायामविशुद्धये॥ ३८॥

**38.** Sitting in the Padmāsana posture, and performing the adoration of the Guru, etc., as taught by the Teacher, let him perform purification of Nāḍīs for success in Prāṇāyāma.

वायुबीजं ततो ध्यात्वा धूम्रवर्णं सतेजसम्।
चन्द्रेण पूरयेद्वायुं बीजं षोडशकैः सुधीः॥ ३९॥
चतुःषष्ट्या मात्रया च कुम्भकेनैव धारयेत्।
द्वात्रिं शन्मात्रया वायुं सूर्यनाड्या च रेचयेत्॥ ४०॥

**39–40.** Contemplating on Vāyu-Bīja (*i.e.,* **यं**), full of energy and of a smoke-colour, let him draw in breath by the left nostril, repeating the Bīja sixteen times. This is Pūraka. Let him restrain the breath for a period of sixty-four repetitions of the Mantra. This is Kumbhaka. Then let him expel the air by the right nostril slowly during a period occupied by repeating the Mantra thirty-two times.

नाभिमूलाद्वह्निमुत्थाप्य ध्यायेत्तेजोऽवनीयुतम्।
वह्निबीजषोडशेन सूर्यनाड्या च पूरयेत्॥ ४१॥
चतुःषष्ट्या मात्रया च कुम्भकेनैव धारयेत्।
द्वात्रिंशन्मात्रया वायुं शशिनाड्या च रेचयेत्॥ ४२॥

**41–42.** The root of the navel is the seat of Agni-Tattva. Raising the fire from that place, join the Pṛthivī-Tattva with it; then contemplate on this mixed light. Then repeating sixteen times the Agni-Bīja (**रं**), let him draw in breath by the right nostril, and retain it for the period of sixty-four repetitions of the Mantras, and then expel it by the left nostril for a period of thirty-two repetitions of the Mantra.

**नासाग्रे शशधृग्बिम्बं ध्यात्वा ज्योत्स्नासमन्वितम्।**
**ठं बीजंषोडशेनैव इडया पूरयेन्मरुत्॥ ४३॥**
**चतुःषष्ट्या मात्रया च वं बीजेनैव धारयेत्।**
**अमृतं प्लावितं ध्यात्वा नाडीधौतं विभावयेत्।**
**लकारेण द्वात्रिंशेन दृढं भाव्यं विरेचयेत्॥ ४४॥**

**43–44.** Then fixing the gaze on the tip of the nose and contemplating the luminous reflection of the moon there, let him inhale through the left nostril, repeating the Bīja ṭham (**ठं**) sixteen times; let him retain it by repeating the Bīja (**ठं**) sixty-four times; in the meanwhile imagine (or contemplate) that the nectar flowing from the moon at the tip of the nose runs through all the vessels of the body, and purifies them. Thus contemplating, let him expel the air by repeating thirty-two times the Pṛthivī Bīja laṁ (**लं**).

**एवंविधां नाडीशुद्धिं कृत्वा नाडीं विशोधयेत्।**
**दृढौ भूत्वासनं कृत्वा प्राणायामं समाचरेत्॥ ४५॥**

**45.** By these three Prāṇāyāmas the nāḍīs are purified. Then sitting firmly in a posture, let him begin regular Prāṇāyāma.

**सहितः सूर्यभेदश्च उज्जायी शीतली तथा।**
**भस्त्रिका भ्रामरी मूर्छा केवली चाष्टकुम्भिकाः॥ ४६॥**

KINDS OF KUMBHAKA

**46.** The Kumbhakas or retentions of breath are of eight sorts; Sahita, Sūrya-bheda, Ujjāyī, Śītalī, Bhastrikā, Bhrāmarī, Mūrchā and Kevalī.

**सहितो द्विविधः प्रोक्तः सगर्भश्चनिगर्भकः।**
**सगर्भो बीजमुच्चार्य निगर्भो बीजवर्जितः॥ ४७॥**

1. SAHITA

**47.** The Sahita Kumbhaka is of two sorts :—Sagarbha and Nirgarbha. The Kumbhaka performed by the repetition of Bīja Mantra is Sagarbha; that done without such repetition is Nirgarbha.

प्राणायामं सगर्भं च प्रथमं कथयामि ते।
सुखासने चोपविश्य प्राङ्मुखो वाप्युदङ्मुखः।
ध्यायेद्विधिं रजोगुणं रक्तवर्णमवर्णकम्॥ ४८॥

**48.** First I shall tell thee the Sagarbha Prāṇāyāma. Sitting in Sukhāsana posture, facing east or north, let him contemplate on Brahmā full of Rajas quality of a blood-red colour, in the form of the letter **अ.**

इडया पूरयेद्वायुं मात्रया षोडशैः सुधीः।
पूरकान्ते कुम्भकाद्ये कर्तव्यस्तूड्डीयानकः॥ ४९॥

**49.** Let the wise practitioner inhale by the left nostril, repeating अँ sixteen times. Then before he begins retention (but at the end of inhalation), let him perform Uḍḍīyānabandha.

सत्त्वमयं हरिंध्यात्वा उकारं कृष्णवर्णकम्।
चतुःषष्ट्या च मात्रया कुम्भकेनैव धारयेत्॥ ५०॥

**50.** Then let him retain breath by repeating उ sixty-four times, contemplating on Hari, of a black colour and of Satva quality.

तमोमयं शिवं ध्यात्वा मकारं शुक्लवर्णकम्।
द्वात्रिंशन्मात्रया चैव रेचयेद्विधिना पुनः॥ ५१॥

**51.** Then let him exhale the breath through the right nostril by repeating mam (मँ) thirty-two times, contemplating Śiva of a white colour and of Tamas quality.

पुनः पिङ्गलयापूर्य कुम्भकेनैव धारयेत्।
इडया रेचयेत् पश्चाद् तद्बीजेन क्रमेण तु॥ ५२॥

**52.** Then again inhale through Piṅgalā (right nostril), retain by Kumbhaka, and exhale by Iḍā (1eft), in the method taught above, changing the nostrils alternately.

**अनुलोमविलोमेन वारंवारं च साधयेत्।**
**पूरकान्ते कुम्भकान्तं धृतनासापुटद्वयम्।**
**कनिष्ठानामिकाङ्गुष्ठै तर्जनीमध्यमे विना॥ ५३॥**

**53.** Let him practise, thus alternating the nostrils again and again. When inhalation is completed, close both nostrils, the right one by the thumb and the left one by the ring-finger and little-finger, never using the index and middle-fingers. The nostrils to be closed so long as Kumbhaka is.

**प्राणायामो निगर्भस्तु विना बीजेन जायते।**
**वामजानूपरिन्यस्तवामपाणितलं भ्रमेत्।**
**एकादिशतपर्यन्तं पूरकुम्भकरेचनम्॥ ५४॥**

**54.** The Nirgarbha (or simple or mantraless) Prāṇāyāma is performed without the repetition of Bīja mantra; and the period of Pūraka (inhalation or inspiration), Kumbhaka (retention), and Recaka (expiration), may be extended from one to hundred mātrās.

**उत्तमा विंशतिर्मात्रा षोडशी मात्रा मध्यमा।**
**अधमा द्वादशी मात्रा प्राणायामास्त्रिधा स्मृताः॥ ५५॥**

**55.** The best is twenty Mātrās : *i.e.,* Pūraka 20 seconds, Kumbhaka 80, and Recaka 40 seconds. The sixteen mātrās is middling, *i.e.,* 16, 64 and 32. The twelve mātrās is the lowest, *i.e.,* 12, 48, 24. Thus the Prāṇāyāma is of three sorts.

**अधमाज्जायते घर्मो मेरुकम्पश्च मध्यमात्।**
**उत्तमाच्च भूमित्यागस्त्रिविधं सिद्धिलक्षणम्॥ ५६॥**

**56.** By practising the lowest Prāṇāyāma for sometime, the body begins to perspire copiously; by practising the middling, the body begins to quiver (especially, there is a feeling of quivering along the spinal cord). By the highest Prāṇāyāma, one leaves the ground, *i.e.,* there is levitation. These signs attend the success of these three sorts of Prāṇāyāma.

प्राणायामात् खेचरत्त्वं प्राणायामाद् रोगनाशनम्।
प्राणायामाद्बोधयेच्छक्तिं प्राणायामान्मनोन्मनी।
आनन्दो जायते चित्ते प्राणायामी सुखी भवेत्॥ ५७॥

**57.** By Prāṇāyāma is attained the power of levitation (Khecarī Śakti), by Prāṇāyāma diseases are cured, by Prāṇāyāma the Śakti (spiritual energy) is awakened, by Prāṇāyāma is obtained the calmness of mind and exaltation of mental powers (clairvoyance, etc.); by this, mind becomes full of bliss; verily the practitioner of Prāṇāyāma is happy.

अथ सूर्यभेदकुम्भकः
घेरण्ड उवाच
कथितं सहितं कुम्भं सूर्यभेदनकं शृणु।
पूरयेत् सूर्यनाड्या च यथाशक्ति बहिर्मरुत्॥ ५८॥
धारयेद्बहुयत्नेन कुम्भकेन जलन्धरैः।
यावत् स्वेदं नखकेशाभ्यां तावत् कुर्वन्तु कुम्भकम्॥ ५९॥

2. SŪRAYABHEDA KUMBHAKA

*Gheraṇḍa said*

**58–59.** I have told thee the Sahita Kumbhaka, now hear the Sūryabheda. Inspire with all your strength the external air through the sun-tube (right nostril) : retain this air with the greatest care, performing the Jālandhara Mudrā. Let the Kumbhaka be kept up so long as the perspiration does not burst out from the tips of the nails and the roots of the hair.

प्राणोऽपानः समानश्चोदानव्यानौ तथैव च।
नागः कूर्मश्च कृकरो देवदत्तो धनञ्जयः॥ ६०॥

THE VĀYUS

**60.** The Vāyus are ten, namely Prāṇa, Apāna, Samāna, Udāna and Vyāna; Nāga, Kūrma, Kṛkara, Devadatta and Dhanañjaya.

हृदि प्राणो वहेन्नित्यमपानो गुदमण्डले।
समानो नाभिदेशे तु उदानः कण्ठमध्यगः॥ ६१॥
व्यानो व्याप्य शरीरे तु प्रधानाः पञ्च वायवः।
प्राणाद्याः पञ्च विख्याता नागाद्याः पञ्च वायवः॥ ६२॥

*Their seats*

**61–62.** The Prāṇa moves always in the heart; the Apāna in the sphere of anus; the Samāna in the navel region; the Udāna in the throat; and the Vyāna pervades the whole body. These are the five principal Vāyus, known as Prāṇādi. They belong to the Inner body. The Nāgādi five Vāyus belong to the Outer body.

तेषामपि च पञ्चानां स्थानानि च वदाम्यहम्।
उदगारे नाग आख्यातः कूर्मस्तून्मीलने स्मृतः॥ ६३॥
कृकरः क्षुत्कृते ज्ञेयो देवदत्तो विजृम्भणे।
न जहाति सृते क्वापि सर्वव्यापी धनञ्जयः॥ ६४॥

**63–64.** I now tell thee the seats of these five external Vāyus. The Nāga-Vāyu performs the function of eructation; the Kūrma opens the eye-lids; the Kṛkara causes sneezing; the Devadatta does yawning; the Dhanañjaya pervades the whole gross body, and does not leave it even after death.

नागो गृह्णाति चैतन्यं कूर्मश्चैव निमेषणम्।
क्षुत्तृषं कृकरश्चैव जृम्भणं चतुर्थेन तु।
भवेद्धनञ्जयाच्छब्दं क्षणमात्रं न निःसरेत्॥ ६५॥

**65.** The Nāga-Vāyu gives rise to consciousness, the Kūrma causes vision, the Kṛkara hunger and thirst, the Devadatta produces yawning and by Dhanañjaya sound is produced; this does not leave the body ever.

सर्वे ते सूर्यसंभिन्ना नाभिमूलात् समुद्धरेत्।
ईडया रेचयेत् पश्चाद् धैर्येणाखण्डवेगतः॥ ६६॥
पुनः सूर्येण चाकृष्य कुम्भयित्वा यथाविधि।
रेचयित्वा साधयेत्तु क्रमेण च पुनःपुनः॥ ६७॥

**66–67.** All these Vāyus, separated by the Sūrya-nāḍī, let him raise up from the root of the navel; then let him expire by the Iḍā-nāḍī, slowly and with unbroken, continuous force. Let him again draw the air through the right nostril, retaining it, as taught above, and exhale it again. Let him do this again and again. In this process, the air is always inspired through the Sūrya-nāḍī.

**कुम्भकः सूर्यभेदस्तु जरामृत्युविनाशकः।**
**बोधयेत् कुंडलीं शक्तिं देहानलं विवर्धयेत्।**
**इति ते कथितं चण्ड सूर्यभेदनमुत्तमम्।। ६८।।**

*Its benefits*

**68.** The Sūrya-bheda Kumbhaka destroys decay and death, awakens the Kuṇḍalī śakti, increases the bodily fire. O Caṇḍa! thus have I taught thee the Sūraybhedana Kumbhaka.

*N.B.*—The description of this process, as given in Haṭha-Yoga Pradīpikā, is somewhat different. Soon after Pūraka (inspiration), one should perform Jālandhara and at the end of Kumbhaka, but before Recaka perform the Uḍḍīyānabandha. Then quickly contract the anal orifice by Mūlabandha, contract the throat, pull in the stomach towards the back; by this process the air is forced into the Brahma-nāḍī (Suṣumnā). Raise the Apāna up, lower the Prāṇa, below the Kaṇṭha; a Yogī becom free from decay : the air should be drawn through the right nostril and expelled through the left.

**अथ उज्जायी कुम्भकः**

**नासाभ्यां वायुमाकृष्य मुखमध्ये च धारयेत्।**
**हृद्गलाभ्यां समाकृष्य वायुं वक्त्रे च धारयेत्।। ६९।।**

3. UJJĀYĪ

**69.** Close the mouth, draw in the external air by both the nostrils, and pull up the internal air from the lungs and throat; retain them in the mouth.

मुखं प्रक्षाल्य संवन्द्य कुर्याज्जालन्धरं ततः।
आशक्ति कुम्भकं कृत्वा धारयेदविरोधतः॥ ७०॥

**70.** Then having washed the mouth *(i.e.,* expelled air through mouth) perform Jālandhara. Let him perform Kumbhaka with all his might and retain the air unhindered.

उज्जायीकुम्भकं कृत्वा सर्वकार्याणि साधयेत्।
न भवेत् कफरोगश्च क्रूरवायुरजीर्णकम्॥ ७१॥
आमवातः क्षयः कासो ज्वरप्लीहा न विद्यते।
जरामृत्युविनाशाय चोज्जायीं साधयेन्नरः॥ ७२॥

**71–72.** All works are accomplished by Ujjāyī Kumbhaka. He is never attacked by phlegm diseases, or nervous diseases, or indigestion, or dysentery, or consumption, or cough; or fever or [enlarged] spleen. Let a man perform Ujjāyī to destroy decay and death.

*N.B.*—See the Haṭha-Yoga Pradīpikā, Chap. II—51, 53 for a different description of this.

अथ शीतलीकुम्भकः

जिह्वया वायुमाकृष्य उदर पूरयेच्छनैः।
क्षणं च कुम्भक कृत्वा नासाभ्यां रेचयेत् पुनः॥ ७३॥

4. ŚĪTALĪ

**73.** Draw in the air through the mouth (with the lips contracted and tongue thrown out), and fill the stomach slowly. Retain it there for a short time. Then exhale it through both the nostrils.

सर्वदा साधयेद्योगी शीतलीकुम्भकं शुभम्।
अजीर्णं कफपित्तञ्च नैव तस्य प्रजायते॥ ७४॥

**74.** Let the Yogī always practise this Śītalī Kumbhaka, giver of bliss; by so doing, he will be free from indigestion, phlegm and bilious disorders.

अथ भस्त्रिकाकुम्भकः

भस्त्रैव लोहकाराणां यथाक्रमेण संभ्रमेत्।
तथा वायुं च नासाभ्यामुभाभ्यां चालयेच्छनैः॥ ७५॥

5. BHASTRIKĀ (BELLOW)

**75.** As the bellows of the ironsmith constantly dilate and contract, similarly let him slowly draw in the air by both the nostrils and expand the stomach; then throw it out quickly (the wind making sound like bellows).

एवं विंशतिवारं च कृत्वा कुर्याच्च कुम्भकम्।
तदन्ते चालयेद्वायुं पूर्वोक्तं च यथाविधि॥ ७६॥
त्रिवारं साधयेदेनं भस्त्रिकाकुम्भकं सुधीः।
न च रोगो न च क्लेश आरोग्यं न दिने दिने॥ ७७॥

**76–77.** Having thus inspired and expired quickly twenty times, let him perform Kumbhaka; then let him expel it by the previous method. Let the wise one perform this Bhastrikā (bellows-like) Kumbhaka thrice : he will never suffer any disease and will be always healthy.

अथ भ्रामरीकुम्भकः

अर्धरात्रे गते योगी जन्तूनां शब्दवर्जिते।
कर्णौ पिधाय हस्ताभ्यां कुर्यात् पूरककुम्भकम्॥ ७८॥

6. BHRĀMARĪ OR BEETLE DRONING KUMBHAKA

**78.** At past midnight, in a place where there are no sounds of any animals, etc., to be heard, let the Yogī practise Pūraka and Kumbhaka, closing the ears by the hands.

शृणुयाद्दक्षिणे कर्णे नादमन्तर्गतं शुभम्।
प्रथमं झिञ्झीनादं च वंशीनादं ततः परम्॥ ७९॥
मेघझर्झरभ्रमरी घण्टाकांस्यं ततः परम्।
तुरीभेरमृदङ्गादिनिनादानकदुन्दुभिः॥ ८०॥

**79–80.** He will hear then various internal sounds

in his right ear. The first sound will be like that of crickets, then that of a lute, then that of a thunder, then that of a drum, then that of a beetle, then that of bells, then those of gongs of bell-metal, trumpets, kettle-drums, mṛdaṅga, military drums, and dundubhi, etc.

**एवं नानाविधो नादो जायते नित्यमभ्यसात्।**
**अनाहतस्य शब्दस्य तस्य शब्दस्य यो ध्वनिः॥ ८१॥**
**ध्वनेरन्तर्गतं ज्योति ज्योतिरन्तर्गतं मनः।**
**तन्मनो विलयं याति तद्विष्णोः परमं पदम्।**
**एवं भ्रामरीसंसिद्धिः समाधिसिद्धिमाप्नुयात्॥ ८२॥**

**81–82.** Thus various sounds are cognised by daily practice of this Kumbhaka. Last of all is heard the Anāhata sound rising from the heart; of this sound there is a resonance, in that resonance there is a Light. In that Light the mind should be immersed. When the mind is absorbed, then it reaches the Highest seat of Viṣṇu (parama-pada). By success in this Bhrāmarī Kumbhaka one gets success in Samādhi.

**अथ मूर्च्छाकुम्भकः**

**सुखेन कुम्भकं कृत्वा मनश्च भ्रुवोरन्तरम्।**
**संत्यज्य विषयान् सर्वान् मनोमूर्च्छा सुखप्रदा।**
**आत्मनि मनसो योगादानन्दो जायते ध्रुवम्॥ ८३॥**

7. MŪRCHĀ

**83.** Having performed Kumbhaka with comfort, let him withdraw the mind from all objects and fix it in the space between the two eyebrows. This causes fainting of the mind, and gives happiness. For, by thus joining the Manas with the Ātmā, the bliss of Yoga is certainly obtained.

अथ केवलीकुम्भकः

हंकारेण बहिर्याति सःकारेण विशेत् पुनः।
षट्शतानि दिवारात्रौ सहस्राण्येकविंशतिः।
अजपां नाम गायत्रीं जीवो जपति सर्वदा॥ ८४॥

8. KEVALĪ

**84.** The breath of every person in entering makes the sound of "saḥ" and in coming out, that of "ham." These two sounds make **सोऽहम्** (so'ham "I am That") or **हंसः** (hamsa "The Great Swan"). Throughout a day and a night there are twenty-one thousand and six hundred such respirations, (that is, 15 respirations per minute). Every living being (Jīva) perfoms this japa unconsciously, but constantly. This is called Ajapā gāyatrī.

मूलाधारे यथा हंसस्तथा हि हृदि पङ्कजे।
तथा नासापुटद्वन्द्वे त्रिभिर्हंससमागमः॥ ८५॥

**85.** This Ajapā japa is performed in three places, *i.e.,* in the Mūladhāra (the space between anus and membranum virile), in the Anāhat lotus (heart) and in the Ājñya lotus (the space where the two nostrils join).

षण्णवत्यङ्गुलीमानं शरीरं कर्मरूपकम्।
देहाद्बहिर्गतो वायुः स्वभावाद् द्वादशाङ्गुलिः॥ ८६॥
गायने षोडशाङ्गुल्यो भोजने विंशतिस्तथा।
चतुर्विंशाङ्गुलिः पन्थे निद्रायां त्रिंशदङ्गुलिः।
मैथुने षट्त्रिंशदुक्तं व्यायामे च ततोधिकम्॥ ८७॥

**86–87.** This body of Vāyu is ninety-six digits length *(i.e.,* six feet)as a standard. The ordinary length of the air-current when expired is twelve digits (nine inches); in singing, its length becomes sixteen digits (one foot); in eating, it is twenty digits (15 inches); in walking, it is twentyfour digits (18 inches); in sleep, it is thirty digits (27 ½ inches); in copulation, it is thirty-six digits (27 inches), and in taking physical exercise, it is more than that.

**स्वभावेऽस्य गतेर्न्यूने परमायुः प्रवर्धते।**
**आयुःक्षयोऽधिके प्रोक्तो मारुते चान्तराद्गते॥ ८८॥**

**88.** By decreasing the natural length of the expired current from nine inches to less and less, there takes place increase of life; and by increasing the current, there is decrease of life.

**तस्मात् प्राणे स्थिते देहे मरणं नैव जायते।**
**वायुना घटसम्बन्धे भवेत् केवलकुम्भकम्॥ ८९॥**

**89.** So long as breath remains in the body there is no death. When the full length of the wind is all confined in the body, nothing being allowed to go out, it is Kevala Kumbhaka.

**यावज्जीवं जपेन्मन्त्रमजपासंख्यकेवलम्।**
**अद्यावधि धृतं संख्याविभ्रमं केवलीकृते॥ ९०॥**
**अत एव हि कर्तव्यः केवलीकुम्भको नरैः।**
**केवली चाजपासंख्या द्विगुणा च मनोन्मनी॥ ९१॥**

**90–91.** All Jīvas are constantly and unconsciously reciting this Ajapā Mantra, only for a fixed number of times every day. But a Yogī should recite this consciously and counting the numbers. By doubling the number of Ajapā (*i.e.,* by 30 respirations per minute), the state of Manonmanī (fixedness of mind) is attained. There are no regular Recaka and Pūraka in this process. It is only (Kevala) Kumbhaka.

**नासाभ्यां वायुमाकृष्य केवलं कुम्भकं चरेत्।**
**एकादिकचतुःषष्टिं धारयेत् प्रथमे दिने॥ ९२॥**

**92.** By inspiring air by both nostrils, let him perform Kevala Kumbhaka. On the first day, let him retain breath from one to sixty-four times.

**केवली मष्टधां कुर्याद् यामे यामे दिने दिने।**
**अथवा पञ्चधा कुर्याद् यथा तत् कथयामि ते॥ ९३॥**

प्रातर्मध्याह्नसायाह्ने मध्ये रात्रिचतुर्थके।
त्रिसन्ध्यमथवा कुर्यात् सममाने दिने दिने॥ ९४॥

**93–94.** This Kevalī should be performed eight times a day, once in every three hours; or one may do it five times a day, as I shall tell thee. First in the early morning, then at noon, then in the twilight, then at midnight, and then in the fourth quarter of the night. Or one may do it thrice a day, *i.e.*, in the morning, noon and evening.

पञ्चवारं दिने वृद्धिर्वारैकं च दिने तथा।
अजपापरिमाणं च यावत् सिद्धिः प्रजायते॥ ९५॥
प्राणायामं केवलीं च तदा वदति योगवित्।
केवली कुम्भके सिद्धे किन्न सिद्ध्यति भूतले॥ ९६॥

इति श्रीघेरण्डसंहितायां घेरण्डचण्डसंवादे घटस्थयोगप्रकरणे
प्राणायामप्रयोगो नाम पञ्चमोपदेशः।

**95–96.** So long as success is not obtained in Kevalī, he should increase the length of Ajapā japa every day, one to five times. He who knows Prāṇāyāma and Kevalī is the real Yogī. What can he not accomplish in this world who has acquired success in Kevalī Kumbhaka?

———

# Lesson 6

## षष्ठोपदेशः

## अथ ध्यानयोगः

## Dhyāna Yoga

**घेरण्ड उवाच**

**स्थूलं ज्योतिस्तथा सूक्ष्मं ध्यानस्य त्रिविधं विदुः।**
**स्थूलं मूर्तिमयं प्रोक्तं ज्योतिस्तेजोमयं तथा।**
**सूक्ष्मं बिन्दुमयं ब्रह्म कुण्डलीपरदेवता।। १।।**

GHERAṆḌA SAID

**1.** The Dhyāna or cantemplation is of three sorts: gross, subtle and luminous. When a particular figure, such as one's Guru or Deity is contemplated, it is Sthūla or gross contemplation. When Brahma or Prakṛti is contemplated as a mass of light, it is called Jyotis contemplation. When Brahma as a Bindu (point) and Kuṇḍalī force are contemplated, it is Sūkṣma or Subtle contemplation.

**अथ स्थूलध्यानम्**

**स्वकायहृदये ध्यायेत् सुधासागरमुत्तमम्।**
**तन्मध्ये रत्नद्वीपं तु सुरत्नवालुकामयम्।। २।।**
**चतुर्दिक्षु नीपतरुं बहुपुष्पसमन्वितम्।**
**नीपोपवनसंकुलैर्वेष्ठितं परिखा इव।। ३।।**

मालतीमल्लिकाजातीकैशरैश्चम्पकेस्तथा।
पारिजातैः स्थलपद्मैर्गन्धामोदितदिङ्मुखैः॥ ४॥
तन्मध्ये संस्मरेद्योगी कल्पवृक्षं मनोहरम्।
चतुःशाखाचतुर्वेदं नित्यपुष्पफलान्वितम्॥ ५॥
भ्रमराः कोकिलास्तत्र गुञ्जन्ति निगदन्ति च।
ध्यायेत्तत्र स्थिरो भूत्वा महामाणिक्यमण्डपम्॥ ६॥
तन्मध्ये तु स्मरेद्योगी पर्यङ्कं सुमनोहरम्।
तत्रेष्टदेवतां ध्यायेत्यद्ध्यानं गुरुभाषितम्॥ ७॥
यस्य देवस्य यद्रूपं यथा भूषणवाहनम्।
तद्रूपं ध्यायते नित्यं स्थूलध्यानमिदं विदुः॥ ८॥

1. STHŪLA DHYĀNA

**2–8.** (Having closed the eyes), let him contemplate that there is a sea of nectar in his heart : that in the midst or that sea there is an island of precious stones, the very sand of which is pulverised diamonds and rubies. That on all sides of it, there are Kadamba trees, laden with sweet flowers; that, next to these trees, like a rampart, there is a row of flowering trees, such as mālati, mallikā, jāti, kesara, campaka, pārijāta and padmas, and that the fragrance of these flowers is spread all round, in every quarter. In the middle of this garden, let the Yogī imagine that there stands a beautiful Kalpa tree, having four branches, representing the four Vedas, and that it is full of flowers and fruits. Insects are humming there and cuckoos singing. Beneath that tree, let him imagine a rich platform of precious gems, and on that a costly throne inlaid with jewels, and that on that throne sits his particular Deity, as taught to him by his Guru. Let him contemplate on the appropriate form, ornaments and vehicle of that Deity. The constant contemplation of such a form is Sthūla Dhyāna.

प्रकारान्तरम्

सहस्रारे महापद्मे कर्णिकायां विचिन्तयेत्।
विलग्नसहितं पद्मं द्वादशैर्दलसंयुतम्॥ ९॥
शुक्लवर्णं महातेजो द्वादशैर्बीजभाषितम्।
हसक्षमलवरयुं हसखफ्रें यथाक्रमम्॥ १०॥
तन्मध्ये कर्णिकायां तु अकथादि रेखात्रयम्।
हलक्षकोणसंयुक्तं प्रणवं तत्र वर्तते॥ ११॥

ANOTHER PROCESS

**9–11.** Let the Yogī imagine that in the pericarp of the great thousand-petalled Lotus (Brain) there is a smaller lotus having twelve petals. Its colour is white, highly luminous, having twelve bīja letters, named **ह, स, क्ष, म, ल, व, र युँ, ह, स ख, फ्रें,** (ha sa kṣa ma la va ra yuṁ ha sa kha phrem). In the pericarp of this smaller lotus there are three lines forming a triangle **अ, क थ,** (a ka tha) : having three angles called **ह, ल, क्ष,** (ha la kṣa) : and in the middle of this triangle, there is the Praṇava **ओम्** I Oṁ.

नादबिंदुमयं पीठं ध्यायेत्तत्र मनोहरम्।
तत्रोपरि हंसयुग्मं पादुका तत्र वर्तते॥ १२॥

**12.** Then let him contemplate that in that there is a beautiful seat having Nāda and Bindu. On that seat there are two swans, and a pair of wooden sandals or shoes.

ध्यायेत्तत्र गुरुं देवं द्विभुजं च त्रिलोचनम्।
श्वेताम्बरधरं देवं शुक्लगन्धानुलेपनम्॥ १३॥
शुक्लपुष्पमयं माल्यं रक्तशक्तिसमन्वितम्।
एवंविधगुरुध्यानात् स्थूलध्यानं प्रसिध्यति॥ १४॥

**13–14.** There let him contemplate his Guru Deva, having two arms and two eyes, and dressed in pure white, anointed with white sandal-paste, wearing garlands of white flowers; to the left of whom stands Śakti of blood-red colour. By thus contemplating the Guru, the Sthūla Dhyāna is attained.

**अथ ज्योतिध्यानम्**

**घेरण्ड उवाच**

**कथितं स्थूलध्यानं तु तेजोध्यानं शृणुष्व मे।**
**यद्ध्यानेन योगसिद्धिरात्मप्रत्यक्षमेव च॥ १५॥**

2. JYOTIR DHYĀNA

GHERAṆḌA SAID

**15.** I have told thee the Sthūla Dhyāna; listen now to the contemplation of Light, by which the Yogī attains success and sees his Self.

**मूलाधारे कुण्डलिनी भुजगाकाररूपिणी।**
**जीवात्मा तिष्ठति तत्र प्रदीपकलिकाकृतिः।**
**ध्यायेत्तेजोमयं ब्रह्म तेजोध्यानं परात्परम्॥ १६॥**

**16.** In the Mūlādhāra is kuṇḍalinī, having the form of a serpent. The Jīvātmā is there like the flame of a lamp. Contemplate on this flame as the Luminous Brahma. This is the Tejo Dhyāna or Jyotir Dhyāna.

**प्रकारान्तरम्**

**भ्रुवोर्मध्ये मनेर्ध्वे च यत्तेजः प्रणवात्मकम्।**
**ध्यायेत् ज्वालावतीयुक्तं तेजोध्यानं तदेव हि॥ १७॥**

ANOTHER PROCESS

**17.** In the middle of the two eye-brows, above the Manas, there is a Light consisting of Oṁ. Let him contemplate on this flame. This is another method of contemplation of Light.

अथ सूक्ष्मध्यानम्

घेरण्ड उवाच

तेजोध्यानं श्रुतंचण्ड सूक्ष्मध्यानं शृणुष्व मे।
बहुभाग्यवशाद् यस्य कुण्डली जाग्रती भवेत्॥ १८॥
आत्मना सहयोगेन नेत्ररन्ध्राद्विनिर्गता।
विहरेद राजमार्गे च चञ्चलत्वान्न दृश्यते॥ १९॥

3. SŪKṢMA DHYĀNA

GHERAṆḌA SAID

**18–19.** O Caṇḍa! thou hast heard the Tejo Dhyāna, listen now to the Sūkṣma Dhyāna. When by a great good fortune, the kuṇḍalī is awakened, it joins with the Ātmā and leaves the body through the portals of the two eyes; and enjoys itself by walking in the royal road (Astral Light). It cannot be seen on account of its subtleness and great changeability.

शाम्भवीमुद्रया योगी ध्यानयोगेन सिध्यति।
सूक्ष्मध्यानमिदं गोप्यं देवानामपि दुर्लभम्॥ २०॥

**20.** The Yogī, however, attains this success by performing Śāmbhavī Mudrā, *i.e.*, by gazing fixedly at space without winking. (Then he will see his Sūkṣma Śarīra). This is called Sūkṣma Dhyāna, difficult to be attained even by the Devas, as it is a great mystery.

स्थूलध्यानाच्छतगुणं तेजोध्यानं प्रचक्षते।
तेजोध्यानाल्लक्षगुणं सूक्ष्मध्यानं परात्परम्॥ २१॥

**21.** The contemplation of Light is a hundred times superior to contemplation of Form; and a hundred thousand times superior to Tejo Dhyāna is the contemplation of the Sūkṣma.

इति ते कथितं चण्ड ध्यानयोगं सुदुर्लभम्।
आत्मा साक्षाद भवेद यस्मात्तस्माद्ध्यानं विशिष्यते॥ २२॥

इति श्रीघेरण्डसंहितायां घेरण्डचण्डसंवादे घटस्थयोगे सप्तमसाधने
ध्यानयोगो नाम षष्ठोपदेशः॥

**22.** O Caṇḍa! thus have I told thee the Dhyāna Yoga—a most precious knowledge; for, by it, there is direct perception of the Self. Hence Dhyāna is belauded.

---

# Lesson 7

## सप्तमोपदेशः

## अथ समाधियोगः

## Samādhi Yoga

**घेरण्ड उवाच**

**समाधिश्च परो योगो बहुभाग्येन लभ्यते।**
**गुरोः कृपाप्रसादेन प्राप्यते गुरुभक्तितः॥ १॥**

GHERAṆḌA SAID

**1.** The Samādhi is a great Yoga; it is acquired by great good fortune. It is obtained through the grace and kindness of the Guru, and by intense devotion to him.

**विद्याप्रतीतिः स्वगुरुप्रतीतिरात्मप्रतीतिर्मनसः प्रबोधः।**
**दिने दिने यस्य भवेत् स योगी सुशोभनाभ्यासमुपैति सद्यः॥ २॥**

**2.** That Yogī quickly attains this most beautiful practice of Samādhi, who has confidence (or faith) in knowledge, faith in his own Guru, faith in his own Self; and whose mind (manas) awakens to intelligence from day to day.

घटाद्भिन्नं मनः कृत्वा ऐक्यं कुर्यात् परात्मनि।
समाधिं तं विजानीयान्मुक्तसंज्ञो दशादिभिः॥ ३॥

**3.** Separate the Manas from the body, and unite it with the Paramātmā. This is known as Samādhi or Mukti from all states of consciousness.

अहं ब्रह्म न चान्योऽस्मि ब्रह्मैवाहं न शोकभाक्।
सच्चिदानन्दरूपोऽहं नित्यमुक्तः स्वभाववान्॥ ४॥

**4.** I am Brahma, I am nothing else, the Brahma is certainly I, I am not participator of sorrow, I am Existence, Intelligence and Bliss; always free, of one essence.

शाम्भव्या चैव खेचर्या भ्रामर्या योनिमुद्रया।
ध्यानं नादं रसानन्दं लयसिद्धिश्चतुर्विधा॥ ५॥
पञ्चधा भक्तियोगेन मनोमूर्च्छा च षड्विधा।
षड्विधोऽयं राजयोगः प्रत्येकमवधारयेत्॥ ६॥

**5–6.** The Samādhi is four-fold, *i.e.*, Dhyāna-Samādhi, Nāda-Samādhi, Rasānanda Samādhi, and Laya-Samādhi : respectively accomplished by Śambhavī Mudrā, Khecarī Mudrā, Bhrāmarī Mudrā and Yoni-Mudrā. The Bhakti-Yoga Samādhi is fifth, and Rāja-Yoga Samādhi, attained through Mano-Mūrcchā Kumbhaka, is the sixth form of Samādhi.

अथ ध्यानयोगसमाधिः

शाम्भवीं मुद्रिकां कृत्वा आत्मप्रत्यक्षमानयेत्।
बिन्दुब्रह्ममयं दृष्ट्वा मनस्तत्र नियोजयेत्॥ ७॥

1. DHYĀNA-YOGA SAMĀDHI

**7.** Performing the Śāmbhavī Mudrā perceive the Ātmā. Having seen once the Brahma in a Bindu (point of light), fix the mind in that point.

खमध्ये कुरु चात्मानं आत्ममध्ये च खं कुरु।
आत्मानं खमयं दृष्ट्वा न किञ्चिदपि बाधते।
सदानन्दमयो भूत्वा समाधिस्थो भवेन्नरः॥ ८॥

**8.** Bring the Ātmā in Kha (Ether), bring the Kha (Ether or Space) in the Ātmā. Thus seeing the Ātmā full of Kha (Space or Brahma), nothing will obstruct him. Being full of perpetual bliss, the man enters Samādhi (Trance or Ecstasy).

**अथ नादयोगसमाधिः**

**साधनात्खेचरीमुद्रा रसनोर्ध्वगता यदा।**
**तदा समाधिसिद्धिः स्याद्धित्वा साधारणक्रियाम्॥ ९॥**

2. NĀDA-YOGA SAMĀDHI

**9.** Turn the tongue upwards, closing the wind-passages, by performing the Khecarī Mudrā; by so doing, Samādhi (trance asphyxiation) will be induced; there is no necessity of performing anything else.

**अथ रसनानन्दयोगसमाधिः**

**अनिलं मन्दवेगेन भ्रामरीकुम्भकं चरेत्।**
**मन्दं मन्दं रेचयेद्वायुं भृङ्गनादं ततो भवेत्॥ १०॥**
**अन्तःस्थं भ्रमरीनादं श्रुत्वा तत्र मनो नयेत्।**
**समाधिर्जायते तत्र आनन्दः सोऽहमित्यतः॥ ११॥**

3. RASĀNANDA YOGA SAMĀDHI

**10–11.** Let him perform the Bhrāmarī Kumbhaka, drawing in the air slowly : expel the air slowly and slowly, with a buzzing sound like that of beetle. Let him carry the Manas and place it in the centre of this sound of humming beetle. By so doing, there will be Samādhi and by this, knowledge of 'so' 'ham' (I am That) arises, and a great happiness takes place.

**अथ लयसिद्धियोगसमाधिः**

**योनिमुद्रां समासाद्य स्वयं शक्तिमयो भवेत्।**
**सुशृङ्गाररसेनैव विहरेत परमात्मनि॥ १२॥**

**आनन्दमयः संभूत्वा ऐक्यं ब्रह्मणि सम्भवेत्।**
**अहं ब्रह्मेति चाद्वैतं समाधिस्तेन जायते॥ १३॥**

4. LAYA-SIDDHI YOGA SAMĀDHI

**12–13.** Perform the Yonī-Mudrā, and let him imagine that he is Śakti, and Paramātma is Puruṣa; and that both have been united in one. By this he becomes full of bliss, and realises Aham Brahma, 'I am Brahma.' This conduces to Advaita Samādhi.

**अथ भक्तियोगसमाधिः**

**स्वकीयहृदये ध्यायेदिष्टदेवस्वरूपकम्।**
**चिन्तयेद् भक्तियोगेन परमाह्लादपूर्वकम्॥ १४॥**
**आनन्दाश्रुपुलकेन दशाभावः प्रजायते।**
**समाधिः सम्भवेत्तेन सम्भवेच्च मनोन्मनी॥ १५॥**

5. BHAKTI YOGA SAMĀDHI

**14–15.** Let him contemplate within his heart his special Diety; let him be full of ecstasy by such contemplation, let him shed tears of happiness, and by so doing he will become entranced. This leads to Samādhi and Manon-manī.

**अथ राजयोगसमाधिः**

**मनोमूर्च्छां समासाद्य मन आत्मनि योजयेत्।**
**परात्मनः समायोगात् समाधिं समवाप्नुयात्॥ १६॥**

6. RĀJA YOGA SAMĀDHI

**16.** Performing Manomūrcchā Kumbhaka, unite the Manas with the Ātmā. By this Union is obtained Rāja-Yoga Samādhi.

**अथ समाधियोगमाहात्म्यम्**

**इति ते कथितश्चण्ड समाधिर्मुक्तिलक्षणम्।**
**राजयोगसमाधिः स्यादेकात्मन्येव साधनम्।**
**उन्मनी सहजावस्था सर्वे चैकात्मवाचकाः॥ १७॥**

7. PRAISE OF SAMĀDHI

**17.** O Caṇḍa! thus have I told thee about Samādhi which leads to emancipation. Rāja-Yoga Samādhi, Unmanī, Sahajāvasthā are all synonyms, and mean the Union of Manas with Ātmā.

**जले विष्णुः स्थले विष्णुर्विष्णुः पर्वतमस्तके।**
**ज्वालामालाकुले विष्णुः सर्वं विष्णुमयं जगत्॥ १८॥**

**18.** Viṣṇu is in water, Viṣṇu is in earth, Viṣṇu is on the peak of the mountain; Viṣṇu is in the midst of Volcanic fires and flames : the whole Universe is full of Viṣṇu.

**भूचराः खेचराश्चामी यावन्तो जीवजन्तवः।**
**वृक्षगुल्मलतावल्लीतृणाद्या वारि पर्वताः।**
**सर्वं ब्रह्म विजानीयात् सर्वं पश्यति चात्मनि॥ १९॥**

**19.** All those that walk on land or move in the air, all living and animate creation, trees, shrubs, roots, creepers and grass, etc., oceans and mountains—all, know ye, to be Brahma. See them all in Ātmā.

**आत्मा घटस्थचैतन्यमद्वैतं शाश्वतं परम्।**
**घटाद्विभिन्नतो ज्ञात्वा वीतरागं विवासनम्॥ २०॥**

**20.** The Ātmā confined in the body is Caitanya or Consciousness, it is without a second, the Eternal, the Highest; knowing it separate from body, let him be free from desires and passions.

**एवं मिथः समाधिः स्यात् सर्वसङ्कल्पवर्जितः।**
**स्वदेहे पुत्रदारादिबान्धवेषु धनादिषु।**
**सर्वेषु निर्ममो भूत्वा समाधिं समवाप्नुयात्॥ २१॥**

**21.** Thus is Samādhi obtained, free from all desires. Free from attachment to his own body, to son, wife, friends, kinsmen, or riches; being free from all, let him obtain fully the Samādhi.

तत्त्वं लयामृतं गोप्यं शिवोक्तं विविधानि च।
तेषां संक्षेपमादाय कथितं मुक्तिलक्षणम्॥ २२॥

**22.** Śiva has revealed many Tattvas, such as Laya Amṛta, etc.; of them, I have told thee an abstract, leading to emancipation.

इति ते कथितश्चण्ड समाधिर्दुर्लभः परः।
यं ज्ञात्वा न पुनर्जन्म जायते भूमिमण्डले॥ २३॥
इति श्रीघेरण्डसंहितायां घेरण्डचण्डसंवादे घटस्थयोगसाधने योगस्य सप्तसारे समाधियोगो नाम सप्तमोपदेशः समाप्तः॥

**23.** O Caṇḍa! thus have I told thee of Samādhi, difficult of attainment. By knowing this, there is no rebirth in this Sphere.

---